THE MONKEY IN YOUR WALLET

THE PSYCHOLOGY OF BAD FINANCIAL DECISIONS, AND HOW TO TAKE CONTROL

STUART WELCH

HUTTONS PUBLISHING LTD

ISBN 978-1-918851-04-5

Published by Huttons Publishing Ltd

NOTE

This book is written for general educational and informational purposes. It describes psychological research and general principles, not personalised financial advice, and nothing in it should be treated as a specific recommendation for your own circumstances. Where the book references financial products, decisions or actions, these are illustrative rather than prescriptive. Readers should seek appropriately qualified advice before making significant financial decisions.

INTRODUCTION

Meet Your Monkey

You've done something stupid with money. I know this because everyone has, including me, and including whoever is standing next to you right now looking smug about their investment portfolio.

Maybe you sold in a panic and watched the market recover the following Tuesday. Maybe you're still paying off a sofa on finance and can no longer remember why it seemed urgent to buy the sofa at the time. Maybe you check your pension about as often as you check the smoke alarm, which is to say never, until something starts beeping.

Here's the bit that should make you feel better rather than worse. None of that was really you. Or rather, it was you, but it was a very old, very specific part of you. A part that evolved to worry about leopards and food scarcity, not index funds and interest rates, and which has been quietly running your financial life ever since without so much as a job interview.

I've spent twenty-five years in financial services, starting out as an accountant before moving into running the platforms that advisers and everyday consumers actually use to manage their money. I've watched literally millions of financial decisions happen in real time, not in a survey and not in a lab, but in the wild, where people click the actual button using their actual money. And I've come to a firm conclusion. Most people aren't bad with money because they're stupid or lazy. They're bad with money because their brain was built for an entirely different job, and nobody warned them it would end up in charge of a mortgage.

Here's the part I still find genuinely funny. Scientists have tested this theory on monkeys. Real ones, with tails, in a lab. And they did it using coins.

The monkey with a wallet

At Yale, a team of researchers spent years teaching capuchin monkeys to use money. Not pretend money. Small metal tokens the monkeys could exchange with human traders for pieces of food, through a hole in the wall of their enclosure, like a very small and very furry branch of a very strange bank.

The monkeys got remarkably good at this, remarkably fast. They shopped around. They noticed when the price of grapes dropped and bought more of them. They behaved, in short, like sensible little consumers doing exactly what basic economic theory says a rational shopper should do.

Then the researchers introduced risk. A gamble. A coin toss between winning a bit more food or losing a bit of what they had. And the monkeys stopped being sensible little consumers and started behaving exactly like the worst investor you know. They took wild, unnecessary risks purely to avoid a loss, even when the sums didn't add up. One monkey started stealing tokens from the tray when he thought nobody was looking. Another appeared to trade sex for currency, which the research team, to their eternal credit, described in the driest possible academic language.

The point of all this wasn't to prove that monkeys are foolish with money. It was to prove that we are, and that we always were, long before anyone invented the concept of money in the first place. The mistakes weren't taught to the monkeys and they weren't learned by them either. They were already there, sitting in the wiring, waiting for a token economy to come along and switch them on.

That is the monkey this book is named after. Not a metaphor exactly, or not only a metaphor. A real, tested, peer-reviewed explanation for why you behave the way you do with money, sitting underneath every decision you make, usually without asking your permission first.

Why your brain is the wrong tool for the job

Your brain, roughly speaking, was finished a very long time ago. It was built to manage a small number of concrete, physical, immediate problems. Is there food nearby. Is that a threat. Am I still welcome in this group of forty people I will probably know for my entire life.

It is an extraordinarily good brain for that particular job.

It is a shockingly bad brain for the job it now actually has, which is understanding compound interest, reading a pension statement, and working out whether an app charging you a small monthly fee is quietly draining more from you over thirty years than the free alternative ever would.

Nobody handed your brain that memo. So instead, it does what it has always done. It reaches for the nearest ancient shortcut and applies it to a problem the shortcut was never built for. It treats a falling share price the way it once treated a genuine physical threat, and tells you to panic and run. It treats a small monthly subscription the way it once treated a negligible daily risk, and tells you it doesn't matter. It treats the version of you who will retire in thirty years as a stranger, because as far as your brain is concerned, he or she basically is one.

This isn't a flaw in you specifically. It's a flaw in the design brief. You were issued a brain that was built for the savannah and then, with no further training, it was put in charge of a retirement account.

Why this isn't just an excuse

I want to be honest with you early, because the rest of this book only works if you trust me to be. Not everything you do wrong with money can be blamed on your inner monkey. Some of it is simply that nobody ever explained the rules properly, in language plain enough to actually stick.

So this book draws a careful line. Where the science

genuinely shows a behaviour rooted in ancient wiring, shared with monkeys who have never seen a bank statement in their lives, I'll show you the study and let you draw your own conclusions. Where it doesn't, I'll say so plainly, because pretending your DNA is responsible for every bad decision you've ever made would be letting you off far too easily, and letting the industry off far too lightly.

Which brings me to the second half of this book's argument, and the one I find most interesting of all.

The monkeys on the other side of the counter

Here's a twist worth sitting with for a moment. The people designing the credit card statement, the insurance add-on, the four easy payments, the investment platform you use every day, are not evil geniuses in a lair somewhere, rubbing their hands at how gullible you are. They are, for the most part, perfectly decent people trying to build something that works, tested and refined over years against one simple measure. Does it get used. Does it convert. Does it feel easy.

And the version that gets used, that converts, that feels easy, is almost never the version aimed at your careful, rational, spreadsheet-building self. It's the version aimed at your monkey, because your monkey is who actually shows up to make the decision. A minimum payment figure printed larger than the total balance isn't there because someone wants to trap you. It's there because, tested against a hundred other versions, it was the one people responded to. Nobody in that meeting necessarily used the words loss aversion or present bias. They just noticed what worked, the same way a market trader notices which fruit sells faster if you stack it a certain way.

I've spent twenty-five years on the inside of that industry, running the platforms that both advisers and everyday consumers use every day, which means I've sat in the rooms where those decisions get made. What I've watched isn't a conspiracy. It's a feedback loop. A design gets built, it performs well because it happens to fit the shape of the monkey brain on the other end of the screen, and it gets kept, refined and rolled out further, often without anyone stopping to ask exactly why it worked so well in the first place. The industry isn't necessarily plotting against your instincts. It's stumbled into speaking their language fluently, then kept talking simply because the conversation was going so well.

That distinction matters, and it's one I intend to keep making throughout this book. Understanding how a product has been shaped to fit your monkey doesn't require anyone behind the counter to be the villain. It just requires you to recognise the shape when you see it, so you can decide for yourself whether it's a shape that actually suits you.

Where we're going

This book is built in four parts, and I'd encourage you to read them in order at least once, because each one leans on the last.

Part One explains where your monkey came from and why it's still running the show, several hundred thousand years after it stopped being useful for anything except catching a bus. You'll meet the actual experiment behind this book's title, the one that turned an entertaining question into a properly tested scientific finding, and you'll come away understanding exactly why a brain built for a savannah struggles so badly with a mortgage.

Part Two takes you through the monkey in action, chapter by chapter, each one built around a single documented bias rather than a vague feeling that humans are irrational. Why you can't seem to save, no matter how many times you promise yourself you'll start next month. Why you held that terrible investment for three years too long, quietly waiting for it to claw its way back to what you originally paid. Why you spend more the moment your neighbour buys a new car, even though your own perfectly good one hasn't changed at all. One chapter in this part is deliberately different from the rest. It's the one where I tell you a particular bad habit has no monkey behind it whatsoever, and that one is entirely on you, because a book that blames everything on biology isn't offering insight, it's offering an excuse.

Part Three turns the same lens outward. Having spent Part Two learning to spot your own monkey, you'll start spotting him at work behind the products, marketing and small print you deal with every day, put there not by design exactly, but because that's what tends to survive when a product gets tested on real people over and over again. You'll meet a second monkey here too, the one standing on the other side of the counter, and I think you'll find him considerably more sympathetic than you might expect.

Part Four is the practical part, and honestly the one I most want you to actually use rather than simply read. Not willpower, because willpower is a terrible long-term strategy against millions of years of evolution. Systems instead. The kind of small, boring, automatic guardrails that take the monkey out of the decision entirely, so you don't have to win the argument with him every single time, at eleven o'clock at night, tired, with your defences already down.

By the end, I don't expect you to have stopped being a monkey. Nobody manages that. What I do expect is that you'll recognise him the moment he shows up, wallet in hand, absolutely certain he knows what he's doing.

He doesn't. But now, at least, you'll know it's him and not you.

CHAPTER 1
THE BRAIN YOU DIDN'T CHOOSE

Picture a fairly ordinary Tuesday evening. You're on the sofa, phone in hand, half watching something on television, and a notification arrives telling you your portfolio is down for the day. Not by very much. A few percentage points, the kind of movement that happens most weeks and means almost nothing over a thirty year horizon. And yet something in your chest tightens anyway, a small, specific discomfort entirely out of proportion to what's actually happened, which is that a number on a screen has become a slightly smaller number for a few hours.

Now picture a different moment from the same week. Your pension statement arrives in the post, or more likely sits unopened in an app you haven't checked in months, showing a retirement date some three decades away and a projected balance that, if you're honest, you've never really sat down and imagined spending. No notification interrupts your evening for this one. No small tightening in the chest. Just a document, filed away, unread, representing a genuinely enormous decision about your own future that somehow never manages to feel urgent at all.

Here's the strange part, worth pondering on before we go any further. The market dip will very likely have corrected itself by the time you've finished reading this chapter. The unopened pension statement represents a decision that will shape whether you can actually stop working one day, comfortably, on your own terms. And yet one of these got your full attention within seconds, and the other gets filed away for another year, or another decade, without so much as a flicker of urgency attached to it.

This isn't a personal failing unique to you on that particular Tuesday evening. It's the entire subject of this chapter, playing out in miniature, exactly the way it plays out in millions of living rooms every single week. Your brain responded instantly and forcefully to a small, immediate, visible change, and almost not at all to a vastly larger, slower, invisible one. If that pattern sounds backwards, it's because it is, measured against what would actually serve your financial life best. It only makes sense once you understand exactly where that pattern came from, which is where this chapter properly begins.

Here's a question worth asking yourself honestly. If you were designing a brain from scratch, specifically for the job of managing a modern financial life, what would you build in to your creation?

You'd probably want something that could hold a number steady in its head for thirty years without getting bored of it. Something that treated money spent on a Tuesday exactly the same as money spent on a Friday, rather than caring, quite unreasonably, which day of the week it happened to be. Something that could look at a graph showing your pension balance rising by four per cent a year and feel the appropriate level of calm satisfaction, rather than nothing at all, because four per cent a year looks, to the naked eye, suspiciously like a flat line.

You would not, under any circumstances, build a brain that panics at the sight of a red number on a screen. You would not build one that treats a small monthly subscription as beneath its notice, while treating a single annual bill of the exact same total cost as a crisis, purely because one arrives in twelve painless instalments and the other arrives all at once. And you almost certainly wouldn't build one that struggles to care about a person who will retire in thirty years' time, on the grounds that the person in question feels suspiciously like a stranger.

Unfortunately, nobody designed your brain for this job. It came finished, several hundred thousand years ago, built for an entirely different set of problems, and you were handed it at birth with no manual, no warranty, and absolutely no cooling off period.

The job it was actually built for

For almost the entirety of human history, the problems worth solving were physical, immediate and countable on your fingers. Is there food near this water hole. Is that rustling in the grass a predator or the wind. Will the group still let me sit near the fire tonight if I turn up empty handed again. These are the questions your brain evolved to answer, and it became extraordinarily good at answering them, fast, under pressure, usually without conscious thought at all.

Notice what all of those questions have in common. They are concrete. You can see the food, hear the rustle, feel the cold shoulder from the group. They are immediate, arriving and resolving within minutes or hours, not months or decades. And they involve small, manageable numbers. A handful of berries. A few dozen people in your group. Nobody in that environment needed to hold the number four hundred thousand steady in their head and imagine what it might grow to by the time they were sixty five.

Your financial life today asks none of the questions your brain was built to answer, and almost all of the questions it wasn't. It asks you to care about an abstract number on a screen rather than food you can see and touch. It asks you to think in decades rather than hours. And it asks you to hold genuinely enormous figures in your head, compare them sensibly, and act accordingly, which is a bit like asking a calculator built to add single digits to suddenly handle your tax return.

This mismatch has a name among people who study it for a living. They call it evolutionary mismatch, which is a fittingly dry academic term for what is, in practice, a genuinely chaotic situation. You are running twenty first century software on stone age hardware, with no update available, and every so often, entirely predictably, it crashes at the worst possible moment, usually somewhere around the checkout page.

The stranger who will retire in your place

Of all the mismatches, the one that costs people the most money is probably the strangest to explain out loud, so bear with me.

Ask most people whether they care about their future self and they'll say yes, obviously, of course they do. And yet ask that same person to skip a takeaway this week in order to give their sixty five year old self a slightly larger pension, and watch how quickly the enthusiasm cools. This isn't hypocrisy. It's something closer to biology. Brain imaging studies have found that when people think about their future self, the parts of the brain that light up look remarkably similar to the parts that light up when they think about a completely different person. Not a slightly older version of themselves. A stranger.

Which means, in a very real sense, that when you decide whether to save for retirement, you are being asked to make a sacrifice today for the benefit of someone your own brain doesn't entirely believe is you. It's a bit like being asked to work overtime so that a distant cousin you've never met can have a nicer holiday. Technically generous. Not exactly urgent. And that cousin, unhelpfully, is the only one who'll actually be around to enjoy your pension.

Researchers refer to the general pattern here as temporal discounting, or occasionally hyperbolic discounting if you want the version that sounds better at a dinner party. The idea is simple enough. A reward available right now feels disproportionately more valuable than the same reward, or even a larger one, available later. Offer someone a modest sum today or fifty per cent more of it in a month's time, and a striking number will take the smaller sum immediately, despite genuinely more money being on the table for the price of a short wait.

This isn't a uniquely human failing either, which is where the monkeys come back into the story. Researchers studying monkeys have found the same pattern, monkeys reliably preferring a smaller reward now over a larger one shortly afterwards, discounting the value of the future reward steeply the moment any delay is introduced. It's worth noting, in fairness, that scientists still argue about exactly what's driving this in monkeys. Some researchers think it's genuine impatience. Others suspect part of it is simply that the animals forget, during the delay, quite how good the later reward was going to be. Which is a more forgiving explanation but not necessarily a more comforting one for anybody relying on their own memory to save consistently for a pension.

Either way, the practical result for you is the same. The version of you who exists thirty years from now, drawing a pension, is not someone your brain treats as a priority today. He or she is, financially speaking, a stranger you've been quietly asked to fund.

Numbers you cannot actually feel

There's a second mismatch that explains an enormous amount of ordinary, everyday financial chaos, the kind that has nothing to do with pensions or retirement at all.

Your brain is extremely good at noticing things it can see, touch or count directly. A pile of ten apples registers instantly and accurately. A precise, multi-digit number sitting on a banking app does not register in anything like the same way. It has to be processed, translated, understood in the abstract, and abstract processing is slow, effortful and very easy to skip entirely if you're tired, distracted or simply not in the mood.

This is a large part of why contactless payment feels so painless compared with handing over cash. Physical money involves a small, real loss you can watch happen, notes leaving your hand and someone else's hand closing around them. A tap on a card involves no visible loss at all. The money still leaves your account, obviously, but your brain, which evolved to register loss through the senses rather than through a database update, barely notices it happened. Several studies bear this out plainly. People reliably spend more using cards than they do using cash for identical purchases, and the effect gets stronger the more abstract the payment method becomes.

It's also why budgeting is so much harder in practice than it sounds in principle. On paper, budgeting is simple arithmetic. Money in, money out, the difference is what you can spend. In practice, it requires you to mentally aggregate dozens of small, abstract, barely felt transactions across weeks or months into a single meaningful total, which is exactly the kind of task your brain was never built to do quietly in the background. A pile of apples, you can count at a glance. Fourteen separate contactless taps over a fortnight, each one individually forgettable, adding up to a genuine problem, you generally cannot.

Try this for yourself, honestly, before reading any further. Without checking, estimate how much you spent last month on coffee, snacks, small takeaways, anything that felt too minor to think about at the time. Most people, when they actually go back and add it up properly, find the real figure comes as a genuine surprise, usually higher than their instinctive guess, sometimes considerably so. This isn't because you're careless with money. It's because your brain was handling each of those small transactions in complete isolation, the way it would have handled small, low stakes decisions on the savannah, one berry at a time, never once asked to hold the running total of an entire month in view at once. Ask a monkey to track fourteen separate small foraging decisions across a fortnight and add them into a single meaningful sum, and you'd get exactly the same blank stare you'd get from most people asked to do the same with a bank statement. It isn't a skill either of you was ever equipped with.

Why none of this is really your fault, and why that still isn't the whole story

I'll be blunt about where this leaves you, because I think you deserve the blunt version rather than the comforting one.

None of the mismatches in this chapter are personal failings. Nobody sat you down and taught you to discount your future self, any more than anyone taught the Yale capuchins to discount theirs. It's wiring, inherited rather than chosen, and getting angry at yourself for having it makes about as much sense as getting angry at yourself for needing to blink.

But understanding where the wiring came from is only the first half of the job, and I don't want you finishing this chapter thinking that's the whole of it. Knowing why you do something is not the same as being excused from doing anything about it. A pilot who understands exactly why turbulence happens still has to fly the plane through it, and nobody boards a flight reassured purely by the pilot's grasp of meteorology. The rest of this book is about exactly that. First, in the chapters ahead, seeing precisely how this ancient wiring shows up in your everyday financial life, in enough specific, recognisable detail that you'll start spotting it in yourself within days. And then, once you can see it clearly, learning what to actually do about it, because recognising the monkey and outsmarting him turn out to be two entirely different skills.

We'll start, in the next chapter, with the experiment that proves all of this beyond reasonable doubt. A room full of monkeys, a pile of coins, and a discovery that changed how an entire generation of economists thought about human nature.

CHAPTER 2
THE MONKEY MARKETPLACE

Shortly after the turn of the second millennium, a small team of researchers at Yale set out to answer a question that sounds like the start of a joke and turns out to be one of the more important experiments in behavioural economics. Could a monkey learn to use money.

Not learn to want food, obviously. Every animal on the planet manages that without any help from a research grant. The question was narrower and stranger than that. Could a monkey grasp the entirely artificial idea of a token, worthless in itself, that stands in for something it actually wants, can be traded, saved, spent, and reasoned about the way we reason about a coin in our pocket. Money, in other words, isn't food. It's an idea about food, one step removed, and nobody was sure an animal brain could make that leap at all.

The team, led by the economist Keith Chen and the psychologist Laurie Santos, built something they ended up calling the monkey marketplace. A group of capuchin monkeys, already living in a colony at Yale, were given access to a separate enclosure fitted with small holes in the wall. Through those holes, human traders would stand and offer food in exchange for a token, a small metal disc with a hole punched through the middle, not entirely unlike a coin. Each monkey was issued a modest supply of these tokens, kept in a small dish the research team, with a nice bit of restraint, referred to as the monkey's wallet.

Teaching a monkey to shop

It took the monkeys a fair while to understand what was being asked of them. This wasn't instinctive behaviour. Nothing in a monkey's evolutionary history prepared it for the concept of handing over an object in exchange for a completely unrelated one, on trust, with a stranger, based purely on the idea that the object had value because everyone had silently agreed it did. The training itself took weeks, sometimes months, with researchers gradually shaping the behaviour, first simply getting a monkey comfortable holding a token at all, then rewarding the earliest accidental hand offs, then slowly building toward a reliable, repeatable trade. That timeline matters, because it tells you something important before the results even arrive. This wasn't a trick performed by one unusually gifted animal. It was a genuine capacity, built up gradually across a proper sample of monkeys, none of whom had any prior exposure to anything resembling money, tested rigorously enough to survive peer review in a serious academic journal rather than simply making for a good story.

Eventually, though, and this is the first genuinely remarkable part of the story, they got it. They learned to take a token from their dish, pass it through the hole to a trader, and receive a piece of food in return. Trade had arrived in the colony.

Once the monkeys understood the basic mechanic, the researchers began testing something more interesting than whether they could shop. They wanted to know whether the monkeys could shop well.

So they varied the price. On some days, a token bought one piece of apple. On other days, the same token bought two. Basic economic theory predicts that a rational shopper, faced with a price drop, should buy more of the now cheaper good, and shift their spending toward it. This is the kind of prediction that sounds obvious written down and turns out to be genuinely difficult to demonstrate cleanly, even in humans, because human shopping is tangled up with habit, brand loyalty, mood and a hundred other things that have nothing to do with price.

The monkeys, it turned out, didn't have any of that baggage. When apple got cheaper, they bought more apple. When the price of a different food rose, they bought less of it and switched toward whatever was now the better deal. Across a series of these price shift experiments, the capuchins behaved like textbook rational consumers, tracking price changes accurately and adjusting their spending sensibly in response. It was, by any reasonable measure, a genuinely impressive performance from an animal that had only been trading for money for a matter of months.

This part of the story matters more than it might seem at first glance, because it rules out the easiest explanation for what happens next. The monkeys weren't confused about money. They weren't randomly mashing buttons and getting lucky. They understood price, value and trade well enough to shop rationally when the choices were straightforward. Which makes what happened when the choices stopped being straightforward considerably harder to explain away.

Where it goes wrong

The researchers introduced risk. Rather than a fixed, certain price, they offered the monkeys a gamble.

Before looking at what the monkeys actually chose, it's worth understanding how carefully this part of the experiment was built, because the design is what makes the result genuinely persuasive rather than merely suggestive. The two trader options were carefully balanced so that neither one was, on average, a better deal than the other, and which trader offered which framing was rotated and varied across sessions, so the monkeys couldn't simply be responding to a particular trader's face or position rather than the framing itself. The researchers also tracked each monkey's choices across many repeated trials, rather than drawing a conclusion from a handful of lucky or unlucky outcomes, precisely so a run of good or bad luck early on couldn't be mistaken for a genuine underlying preference.

In one version of the test, a monkey could choose a trader who reliably offered one piece of food, but who half the time threw in a bonus second piece for free. Compare that with a different trader who displayed two pieces of food up front, but who half the time took one back before handing anything over. Look closely at the two options and you'll notice something important. They are, mathematically, exactly the same gamble. Both traders offer a fifty per cent chance of one piece and a fifty per cent chance of two. The expected outcome is identical either way.

A purely rational shopper, the kind economists like to imagine populating the world, should feel entirely indifferent between the two. A gain framed as a bonus and an identical gain framed as an avoided loss are, on paper, the same gain. The monkeys were not indifferent. They overwhelmingly preferred the trader offering the possible bonus over the trader who might claw something back, even though the two traders were, in cold economic terms, offering exactly the same deal.

This is the pattern behavioural economists call the reflection effect, and it sits on top of a deeper phenomenon called loss aversion, arguably the single most well documented bias in the whole field. The idea, first properly described in humans by the psychologists Daniel Kahneman and Amos Tversky, is that losses and gains of identical size are not treated as equal by the mind. A loss hurts more than an equivalent gain feels good, and by a meaningful margin too, with much of the research putting a loss at somewhere around twice as painful as an equivalent gain is pleasant. The monkeys, without ever having read a word of Kahneman and Tversky, appeared to feel exactly the same way.

This matters enormously for the argument of this whole book. Loss aversion in humans could, in theory, be a learned response. Something absorbed from a culture that fears financial ruin, or from painful personal experience, or from watching parents flinch at a bill. The capuchins had none of that. They had never seen a bank statement, never lost a job, never watched a parent worry about rent. They had a few months of experience trading tokens for apple in a lab. And they still displayed the same lopsided emotional weighting of gains and losses that shows up reliably in human investors deciding whether to sell a falling share.

The most reasonable conclusion, and the one the research team themselves drew, is that this particular quirk isn't cultural or learned at all. It's wired in at a much deeper level, old enough to be shared across species that split from a common ancestor tens of millions of years ago. Which means that when you catch yourself holding onto a bad investment two years too long, quietly hoping it will claw its way back to what you originally paid, you are not being weak, foolish or badly educated about markets. You are behaving exactly the way a small, food motivated capuchin monkey behaves when offered a gamble involving apple. The wiring predates the wallet by several million years.

The monkey who started stealing

The experiments produced a few other findings worth noting, partly because they're genuinely funny and partly because they show quite how far this rabbit hole goes.

The monkeys also displayed something economists call the endowment effect, the tendency to value something more highly purely because you already own it, rather than because of any change in the object itself. Humans do this constantly. It's why people ask more to sell something than they'd be willing to pay to buy the identical item fresh, and why swapping one lottery ticket for another that has exactly the same odds feels, irrationally, like a bad trade. The Yale capuchins showed the same pattern once they'd been given a token or a food item to hold, valuing it more than an identical item they didn't yet possess.

The follow up study built to test this properly, rather than simply noticing it in passing, gave monkeys a food item to hold for a short period, then offered them the chance to trade it for a different food item, one the same monkeys had shown, in earlier, entirely separate trials, that they valued roughly equally on average. If ownership genuinely had no effect on value, trading should have happened close to half the time in each direction, monkeys occasionally preferring to keep what they had, occasionally preferring to switch, roughly balanced across the group. That isn't what happened. Once an item had been placed in a monkey's possession, even briefly, trading it away for the supposedly equivalent alternative became noticeably less common than the earlier, no ownership trials would have predicted. Something about simply holding the item had measurably shifted how much it was worth to the monkey holding it, in a way that had nothing to do with the item itself, since it was, by design, functionally identical to the one on offer in exchange.

And then there was the monkey who started stealing. During one phase of the research, an observant capuchin worked out that the mesh separating the trading enclosure from the rest of the colony had a gap large enough to slip a paw through, and began quietly lifting tokens from the tray before any trading had officially begun. It's a small detail, almost a footnote in the published research, but it tells you something useful. Given the right incentive structure, even a monkey will find the loophole. Which should perhaps lower your expectations slightly of how virtuous humans are likely to be when a financial product is deliberately built with loopholes of its own, a subject we'll return to properly in Part Three.

An honest complication

I promised at the start of this book that I'd draw an honest line between what the science genuinely supports and what it doesn't, and this chapter is the right place to make good on that promise, because the loss aversion finding, impressive as it is, hasn't gone entirely unchallenged.

A later group of researchers reanalysed the original data and offered a different explanation. Rather than true loss aversion, they argued the monkeys' preferences might be better explained by something called delay of reinforcement, essentially a difference in how quickly and reliably the reward arrived after the choice was made, rather than a genuine emotional weighting of gains against losses. It's a more technical, less headline friendly explanation, and it's fair to say the debate hasn't been fully settled either way.

I mention this not to undermine the finding, which remains widely cited and broadly accepted, but because a book asking you to trust its evidence should be honest about where that evidence gets argued over by the people who produced it. Real science looks like this. Messy, contested, revised, argued about at length by people who have devoted entire careers to a single monkey with a wallet. It's a rather more interesting picture than the tidy, settled version you sometimes get in books that would rather not complicate a good story.

What this means for you

Strip away the academic detail and the conclusion is a simple, slightly uncomfortable one. The tendency to feel losses more sharply than equivalent gains, to prefer a possible bonus over an identical possible clawback, to value something more simply because it's already yours, none of it appears to be something you picked up along the way. It looks like it was there from the start, sitting in wiring old enough to predate the wheel, the written word, and certainly the entire modern financial services industry.

This is the foundation the rest of Part Two builds on. Chapter by chapter, we're going to take that same wiring and follow it into the specific, recognisable corners of your financial life where it actually costs you money. Why you can't quite bring yourself to sell a losing investment. Why a subscription renews quietly for years past the point you actually wanted it. Why watching your neighbour buy a new car makes your own perfectly good one feel suddenly inadequate.

None of it will be your fault in the way you've perhaps assumed it was. But as I said in the last chapter, and I'll keep saying it, understanding where the wiring came from is only ever step one. What you do once you can see it clearly is a different matter entirely, and it's the one this whole book is really about, from here to the very last page.

CHAPTER 3
THE PAIN OF LOSING

You've already met this monkey. He was in the last chapter, trading tokens for apple, flinching at the thought of a clawback even when the maths said he shouldn't bother. I won't reintroduce him properly a second time. Instead, I want to show you where he's been hiding in your own financial life, often in places you'd never have thought to look for him.

The investment you can't quite sell

Start with the one many people recognise immediately. Somewhere in your portfolio, or in a drawer, or in a forgotten app you haven't opened in a while, there's probably an investment doing badly that you bought at a higher price and have never quite managed to bring yourself to sell.

You know, rationally, that the sensible question is simple. Would I buy this today, at today's price, knowing what I know now. If the answer is no, the honest move is to sell it and put the money somewhere better. And yet an enormous number of people hold on regardless, waiting, often for years, for the investment to crawl back up to the exact price they originally paid, as though the market owes them this specific, personal favour.

The price you paid is not information. It has no bearing whatsoever on what the investment is worth today or what it's likely to do tomorrow. But your monkey doesn't treat it as irrelevant history. He treats it as a line in the sand, the point at which selling stops feeling like a sensible decision and starts feeling like admitting defeat. Locking in a loss feels different from watching one sit there unrealised, even though the damage to your wealth is identical either way, to the last decimal point. One is a paper cut you can choose not to look at. The other is a wound you have to actively open yourself. Small wonder people put it off.

There's a particularly stubborn version of this that shows up around funds and shares linked to a person's former employer, or a company they feel some loyalty toward. The emotional cost of selling gets tangled up with a sense of betrayal or admission, on top of the ordinary loss aversion already at play, and the holding period stretches from months into years. I've watched this happen more times than I can count, always with the same quiet justification. It'll come back. Sometimes it does. Often, by the time it does, the money would have grown considerably more sitting somewhere else in the meantime.

The insurance you don't need, and the cover you skip

Loss aversion doesn't only make you hold onto things too long. It also makes you spend money protecting against losses that were never statistically likely, while leaving genuinely serious risks almost entirely uncovered. The pattern looks contradictory until you realise both halves are driven by exactly the same wiring.

Consider extended warranties on electronics, a product that survives almost entirely on loss aversion rather than sound mathematics. The insurer has already priced the policy so that, on average, across every customer who buys one, they come out ahead. That's not a conspiracy, it's just how insurance has to work in order to exist at all. But the individual loss being protected against, a broken laptop screen, a faulty washing machine motor, is vivid, specific and easy to picture, which makes it feel far more threatening than the maths actually justifies. You can practically see the crack forming. That vividness is doing all the work.

Now compare that with something like income protection insurance, which covers the far larger and more statistically significant risk of losing your ability to earn an income at all, through illness or injury. This is, for most people, one of the biggest genuine financial risks they carry. And yet it remains one of the most under-purchased forms of cover there is, largely because the risk it protects against is abstract, unlikely to happen this particular month, and hard to picture vividly at eleven o'clock on a Tuesday night while renewing insurance online. Nobody can see the injury that hasn't happened yet. So the monkey, who only responds to what he can vividly imagine losing, stays quiet, and the policy goes unbought.

Put simply, you end up over-insured against small, vivid, easily imagined losses and under-insured against large, abstract, statistically real ones. Not because you did the sums badly. Because the version of loss your brain responds to was never really about the sums in the first place.

Cash under the mattress, or close enough

The final version of this is quieter than the other two, and arguably more expensive over a lifetime, precisely because it never feels like a decision at all.

Holding money in cash feels safe. Nothing dramatic ever happens to a savings balance sitting in an ordinary account. The number doesn't fall on a bad news day, doesn't wobble when a headline mentions market turmoil, doesn't require you to watch anything happen at all. For a brain wired to fear visible, immediate loss above almost everything else, that stillness feels like the responsible choice.

Except money sitting in cash over long periods is being eroded the entire time by inflation, which quietly reduces what that same pile of money can actually buy, year after year, without a single number on the screen ever moving in the wrong direction. It's a real loss. It's arguably a more certain loss, over a long enough time-frame, than the ordinary ups and downs of a diversified investment. But it's invisible. There's no red arrow, no dramatic dip on a graph, nothing for your monkey to flinch at. So the loss goes entirely unfelt, right up until the day you actually try to spend the money and discover it doesn't stretch nearly as far as you assumed it would.

This is loss aversion working exactly backwards from how you'd expect, and it's a useful reminder of the rule underneath all three examples in this chapter. Your monkey doesn't respond to actual risk. He responds to visible, vivid, immediate risk, and he's almost entirely blind to the slow, quiet, statistically real kind. Markets feel dangerous because you can watch them move. Inflation feels safe because you can't.

The shared account nobody wants to close

One final version of this deserves a mention, because it shows up at some of the most emotionally difficult moments in a person's financial life, and the ordinary loss aversion driving it often goes completely unrecognised in the middle of everything else that's happening.

When a long relationship ends, whether through separation, divorce, or simply a shared household breaking apart, there's often a joint account, a joint investment, or a shared property that needs to be divided or closed. The rational move is very often to settle it cleanly and promptly, agree a fair split, and move both parties on to their own separate financial footing as quickly as reasonably possible. What actually happens, more often than not, is that the account lingers, sometimes for years, neither party quite willing to formally close it, formally sell the shared investment, or formally divide the property, because doing so requires actively, deliberately locking in a loss, whether that loss is financial, emotional, or simply the loss of a shared history the account represents.

This isn't really about the money in most cases. It's the same mechanism as the unsold losing investment from earlier in this chapter, dressed in considerably more painful clothing. Leaving the account open, untouched, unresolved, feels like postponing a loss rather than accepting one. Closing it feels like making that loss official, real, and irreversible, in a way that simply continuing to avoid the decision never quite does. The financial cost of this delay is often substantial, an account earning poor interest, a shared property accruing costs neither party is tracking properly, a joint investment nobody is actively managing. But the emotional pull to avoid formally, deliberately triggering the loss tends to win out regardless, for months or years longer than either party would ever recommend to a friend in the same position.

What ties all four together

Look back at the investment you can't sell, the warranty you didn't need, the savings account slowly losing ground to inflation, and the shared account nobody quite gets round to closing, and you'll notice they don't look like the same problem at first glance. One is about holding on too long. One is about buying protection you didn't need. One is about avoiding a decision altogether. One is about a loss too painful to make official. But underneath, it's the identical monkey, running the identical calculation. Is this loss visible. Is it immediate. Can I picture it happening right now, in front of me.

If the answer is yes, he panics, sometimes usefully, often not. If the answer is no, he stays perfectly calm, even when he probably shouldn't. None of that makes you careless or foolish. It makes you exactly as wired as the capuchin who preferred a possible bonus to an identical possible clawback, because a clawback, however small, is a loss he can actually see coming.

The genuinely useful move isn't to try and switch that wiring off, which isn't really an option anyway. It's to notice, deliberately, whenever a financial decision hinges on how vivid or immediate a loss feels rather than on how likely or large it actually is. That single question, asked honestly, would have caught all four examples in this chapter before they cost anyone a penny, or in the last case, before they cost anyone several more years than they needed to spend untangling a life that had, in every other sense, already moved on.

We'll come back to exactly how to build that question into a habit in Part Four. For now, on to the next place this same monkey turns up, one that costs people money in a rather more dramatic and public way than a forgotten extended warranty ever could.

CHAPTER 4

THROWING GOOD MONEY AFTER BAD

There's a particular sentence that gets said in kitchens, boardrooms and financial advice meetings more often than almost any other, and it's an alarm bell worth learning to hear. I've put too much into this to stop now.

It sounds like wisdom. It sounds like commitment, like seeing something through, like the kind of grit that gets rewarded in the end. It is, in fact, one of the more reliably expensive sentences in the English language, and your inner monkey says it far more often than you'd probably like to admit.

A quick word on what this actually means

The sunk cost fallacy, in its plainest form, is the tendency to keep investing time, effort or money into something because of what you've already put in, rather than because of what you're actually likely to get out of it going forward. The word sunk is doing real work there. Once money is spent, it's gone, permanently, regardless of what you decide to do next. It cannot be brought back by spending more, and it has no bearing whatsoever on whether spending more is now a good idea. And yet it exerts an enormous, entirely irrational pull on the decision anyway.

The rational question, every single time, is forward looking only. Given where I am right now, is putting more in the best use of what I have left. Not, have I already put a lot in. Not, would stopping now mean admitting the earlier spending was wasted. Just, from this exact moment forward, is this still the smart move.

Almost nobody actually asks the question that way, because almost nobody's brain is built to.

The renovation that never quite finishes

Here's a scene I've watched play out more times than I could count, in one form or another. A couple buy a house that needs some work. The kitchen gets done first, on budget, roughly on schedule. Then the bathroom, which runs a bit over. Then, halfway through what was meant to be a modest refresh of the living room, something structural turns up behind a wall that nobody planned for, and the number that started the project bears almost no resemblance to the number now required to actually finish it.

At this point, a genuinely useful question would be whether the remaining work is, priced honestly against what it will cost and what it will actually add to the value or liveability of the house. Very often, by this stage, the honest answer is no, or at least not at this new price. But that's rarely the question that gets asked. The question that actually gets asked is some version of, we've already spent so much, we can't stop now, it'll all have been wasted.

It won't, though. The money already spent is spent regardless of what happens next. Stopping doesn't make the earlier spending more wasted than it already was. Continuing doesn't retroactively make it well spent either. The only genuine question is whether the next amount of money, spent from this point onward, is a good idea on its own terms. Almost nobody frames it that way in the moment, because in the moment, stopping feels like a confession that the whole thing was a mistake, and continuing feels like proof that it wasn't. Neither of those feelings has anything to do with whether continuing is actually, financially, the smart move.

The investment held for entirely the wrong reason

This one sits close to territory we covered in the last chapter, but the mechanism driving it is subtly different, so it's worth separating out properly.

Loss aversion, as we saw in Chapter Three, is about the pain of a loss feeling sharper than the pleasure of an equivalent gain. Sunk cost is a slightly different trap, though the two often show up arm in arm. It's not just that selling at a loss hurts. It's that the amount already invested starts to feel like it obligates you to keep going, as though the size of your prior commitment is itself evidence that the thing must eventually work out.

You'll hear this reasoning almost word for word from people holding a badly performing investment for far too long. I've put five years into this fund, I can't pull out now. I've contributed to this pension for two decades, it feels wrong to move it. The size and duration of the investment gets quietly mistaken for a signal about its future quality, when in reality the two have nothing to do with each other whatsoever. A fund that has performed badly for five years is not somehow owed five more years of your money as a reward for loyalty. It has to earn a place in your portfolio the same way any new investment would, judged from today, on today's terms, with no credit given for history.

The subscription that survives out of guilt

A smaller, quieter version of the same instinct shows up in something almost nobody thinks of as an investment decision at all, the subscriptions and memberships that quietly renew year after year long after their usefulness has faded.

The gym membership barely used past February. The streaming service nobody in the house has opened in months. The professional subscription renewed automatically because cancelling feels like it would somehow waste the money already spent on it, even though that money is entirely gone either way, used or not. Cancelling saves you money starting today. Not cancelling doesn't retrieve a single penny of what's already been spent. But cancelling feels, to the part of the brain running this decision, like admitting the whole thing was a waste from the start, and continuing feels like proof it wasn't. Same trap, much smaller stakes, repeated monthly for years without anyone noticing the total.

The business that should have closed two years ago

Here's a scene I've watched from a rather closer vantage point than some of the others in this chapter, and it's often the most expensive version of sunk cost thinking a person will ever encounter.

A business starts reasonably well, or well enough to justify the initial investment and the early sacrifices that go with starting anything. Then trading gets harder, for whatever reason, a market shift, a stronger competitor, a product that never quite found the audience it was built for. The accounts start telling an increasingly clear story, month after month, of a business that's no longer covering its own costs, propped up instead by savings, a second income, or an increasingly worrying amount of borrowing. Any outside observer looking purely at the numbers would say the same thing fairly quickly. This isn't working, and continuing to fund it isn't a business decision anymore, it's something closer to hope wearing a business decision's clothing.

The owner, understandably, sees something entirely different. Years of their own time. Money already invested, sometimes their entire savings. Relationships, reputation, a sense of identity built around being the person who runs this particular business. Every one of those things is real, and every one of those things is also, in the strict financial sense, already sunk, gone regardless of whatever happens from this point forward. And yet I've sat across from more than one business owner, watching them keep pouring money into a business the accounts had already quietly given up on months earlier, each fresh injection of cash justified by exactly the same reasoning as the renovation earlier in this chapter. We've come this far. We can't stop now.

What makes this version particularly painful, is how much harder the maths gets to see clearly the longer it continues. A business owner drawing down personal savings to fund a failing business isn't just losing the money going in. They're also losing whatever that same money would have earned sitting somewhere else, and very often eroding a personal financial safety net that took years to build, one that a family may need considerably more urgently than the business itself ever did. The sunk cost fallacy doesn't just cost the money already spent. Left unchecked, it quietly recruits everything else nearby too.

Why some of us fall harder than others

There's a genuinely interesting detail buried in the research on this, one that complicates the picture in a useful way rather than tidying it up too neatly.

Studies looking at sunk cost behaviour in monkeys have found the effect in more than one species, capuchins and rhesus macaques both showing a tendency to persist with a task longer the more effort they'd already invested in it, even when persisting no longer made sense. But the two species didn't fall for it equally. Rhesus macaques, generally more repetitive and habitual in how they approach a task, showed the pattern more strongly. Capuchins, generally more willing to experiment and switch strategy mid task, showed it somewhat less.

It's a small detail, but it hints at something bigger. The pull toward sunk cost thinking isn't necessarily a fixed, universal strength. It may be stronger in some temperaments than others, more pronounced in habitual, steady approaches to a problem than in flexible, exploratory ones. Which raises a genuinely useful personal question. Are you, by temperament, more the steady rhesus type or the flexible capuchin type when it comes to your own financial habits. Neither is inherently better. But knowing which one you lean toward tells you exactly where to watch yourself most carefully.

An honest complication

As with loss aversion in Chapter Three, I want to flag that the sunk cost story isn't entirely settled science either, because a book asking for your trust ought to keep being straight with you about where the evidence gets argued over.

Some researchers have pushed back on the sunk cost interpretation of these animal studies altogether, arguing that what looks like irrational persistence might actually be a reasonably sensible strategy under genuine uncertainty. If an animal, or a person, doesn't know for certain how much effort a task will require, continuing after significant investment can sometimes be a rational bet that the end is close, rather than a true fallacy at all. It's a fair point, and it's a useful reminder that not every persistence, in a monkey or in you, is automatically irrational. Sometimes seeing something through really is the right call. The skill, which we'll get to properly in Part Four, is learning to tell the difference between genuinely rational persistence and the version that's really just your monkey refusing to admit the wall came down badly.

The question that actually matters

Every example in this chapter, the renovation, the investment, the subscription, the business kept alive past the point the accounts had already given up on it, collapses down to the same single test, and it's worth writing somewhere you'll actually see it again.

Forget what you've already spent. It's gone either way. Ask only this. From right now, knowing everything I currently know, would I choose to start this, at this price, today. If the honest answer is no, the money already spent isn't a reason to keep going. It's simply the price you've already paid for the lesson, and the lesson is now free. The only question left is whether you're willing to actually use it.

What that actually feels like in the moment is rarely relief. It feels, more often, like admitting a mistake out loud, which is precisely why so few people do it in time. But the alternative isn't neutral either. Every month spent avoiding that admission is another month of good money quietly following bad, and the lesson, already fully paid for, sitting there unused.

CHAPTER 5
EVERYBODY'S DOING IT

There's a particular feeling worth naming properly, because it's done more damage to more portfolios than almost any other single instinct in this book. It's the feeling of watching everyone around you pile into something, and sensing, with real physical discomfort, that you're the only one missing out.

It doesn't feel like a decision when it happens. It feels like catching up. Like finally noticing something everyone else already understood. That feeling is old, useful in its original context, and almost never useful in the one you're applying it to now.

Why copying was once the smartest thing you could do

For nearly all of human history, watching what everyone else was doing and copying it was an excellent survival strategy, arguably one of the best available.

If the rest of your group suddenly ran, working out for yourself, from first principles, whether there was really a predator nearby would have been a luxury you couldn't afford. Running because everyone else was running kept you alive far more reliably than pausing to independently verify the threat.

The same logic applied to food, water and shelter. If everyone in the group had learned, over generations, which berries were safe and which route to the water source avoided a dangerous stretch of ground, copying that knowledge wholesale was vastly more efficient than testing it yourself from scratch. You didn't need to understand why the group avoided a particular tree. You just needed to notice that they did, and do the same.

This tendency, to treat what others are doing as a reliable shortcut for what's true or safe or wise, is called social learning, and it shows up right across the primate world, not just in humans. Researchers studying wild vervet monkeys have documented this directly. In one field experiment, groups of monkeys were taught two different techniques for accessing the same food source. Once individuals had learned one technique, they proved dramatically more likely to go on and learn the second technique too, simply because they'd already seen it demonstrated by others in the group, rather than working it out independently. The researchers also found a clear rank effect. Monkeys were considerably more likely to copy a technique they'd seen a higher ranked individual perform than one demonstrated by a lower ranked group member. Status, in other words, made the behaviour more contagious, not just more visible.

A separate and rather charming piece of field research followed wild vervet troops trained to prefer one colour of maize over another, blue over pink in one group, pink over blue in a neighbouring one. When males migrated between troops, a routine and natural part of vervet social life, they didn't bring their old preference with them. They adopted the new troop's colour preference almost immediately, often on their very first opportunity to feed there, apparently abandoning a food preference they'd held for years the moment the local group demonstrated a different one. The pull to match the group, it turns out, can override even an individual's own prior, direct experience.

None of this is a design flaw. It's a genuinely well engineered piece of evolutionary machinery, built for a world where the group usually did know best, and where independently verifying every piece of shared knowledge would have gotten you killed long before you finished checking.

Where the machinery misfires

Financial markets are, in an important sense, the worst possible environment to run this particular piece of machinery in, because the thing your inner monkey is built to trust, what everyone else appears to be doing, is often the least reliable signal available.

Start with the most dramatic version, a genuine market bubble. Somewhere, an asset starts rising in price. Early buyers, for whatever reason, good analysis or plain luck, do well. Other people notice them doing well. Rather than independently assessing whether the asset is now fairly priced, and it usually isn't, they buy simply because buying appears to be what everyone sensible is currently doing. This drives the price up further, which draws in more buyers on exactly the same reasoning, which drives the price up again. At no point does the underlying value of the asset need to have any relationship whatsoever to what's happening to its price. The whole mechanism runs entirely on the copying instinct, each new buyer treating the previous wave of buyers as evidence, rather than treating the price itself as the thing that actually needs evaluating.

Cryptocurrency cycles over the past decade have followed this pattern almost textbook perfectly, complete with the vivid social proof that makes it so persuasive. A colleague mentions they've made a healthy return. A relative at a family gathering can't stop talking about it. Social media fills with people publicly celebrating gains, and rather less visibly with people quietly not mentioning their losses. None of that constitutes analysis. All of it feels, to the copying instinct inherited from a few million years of group living, like overwhelming and trustworthy evidence.

The same pattern shows up in a quieter, less dramatic form every single year in ordinary fund investing. A fund posts a strong year, sometimes through genuine skill, often partly through luck or a sector having a good run. Money pours in from investors chasing what just performed well, on the entirely understandable but statistically shaky assumption that recent success predicts future success. It very often doesn't. Past performance being no guarantee of future results isn't just a regulatory disclaimer buried in small print. It's a genuinely accurate description of how weakly correlated last year's winning fund is with next year's, and yet the copying instinct treats a strong recent run as exactly the kind of trustworthy group signal it evolved to follow without question.

A street, a queue, and a bidding war

Property markets offer one of the most vivid, physically embodied versions of herding available, because unlike a share price on a screen, you can actually stand in the queue and feel it happening to you in real time.

Picture a viewing on an ordinary house, priced reasonably for its street. On a quiet market, a handful of interested buyers might view it across a week, think it over, make a considered offer close to the asking price. On a rising market, something different happens. The estate agent mentions, entirely truthfully, that several other viewings are booked for the same afternoon. You arrive to find a small queue on the pavement, other buyers, other couples, clearly circling the same property, and something in your assessment of the house itself shifts before you've even opened the front door.

It's not that the house has become more suitable to your needs in the last five minutes. It's that the presence of a queue has been read, instantly and almost involuntarily, as proof the house must be worth having, in exactly the way the copying instinct evolved to read a crowd's behaviour as reliable evidence about a resource worth competing for.

What follows, in a genuinely hot local market, is a bidding process that owes considerably more to the psychology of the queue than to any independent assessment of the property's actual worth. Offers climb not because any individual buyer has done fresh analysis justifying a higher number, but because each new offer functions as fresh social proof that the property is worth exactly that much, which in turn justifies the next offer climbing higher still. Buyers who arrived planning to offer a careful, researched figure leave having offered considerably more, often justifying it afterward with exactly the same reasoning as the fund chaser and the crypto buyer. Everyone else clearly saw something I nearly missed. The queue on the pavement was never information about the house. It was only ever information about how many other people were also, in that exact moment, running the identical copying instinct.

The quiet version, closer to home

Herding doesn't only show up in headline grabbing bubbles. It shows up in smaller, more personal ways too, ones you're less likely to notice happening in the moment.

The financial advice we take from friends and family often carries far more weight than the quality of the advice itself deserves, purely because it comes from someone in our own trusted group. A relative confidently recommending a particular investment, mortgage type or savings approach carries the same rank based persuasive pull the vervet monkeys showed toward higher status individuals, regardless of whether that relative actually knows what they're talking about. Confidence and trust within the group get mistaken for expertise, because for most of human history, within a small stable group, they usually did overlap.

There's a quieter version too, the discomfort of being the only person in your friendship group not participating in something. Everyone else remortgaging to release equity for a renovation. Everyone else moving their savings into the same trending investment app. The discomfort here isn't really about the financial merits of the decision at all. It's the same discomfort the migrating vervet males must have felt on arriving at a troop with an unfamiliar colour preference, an old, deep pull toward matching the group, dressed up in modern clothing as a financial choice.

The workplace produces its own reliable version of the same pattern, one that rarely gets recognised for what it is in the moment. A pension scheme's default contribution rate quietly becomes, for a great many employees, the actual contribution rate, adopted not through any considered assessment of what they personally need for retirement, but because it's what everyone else at the company appears to be doing, and a default that most colleagues have simply accepted starts to feel, entirely without evidence, like the sensible, socially validated choice. The same pattern shows up around share save schemes, additional benefits, and even the general financial culture of a workplace. A team that talks openly about aggressive investing produces more aggressive investors, and a team that never discusses money at all produces employees who never quite get round to reviewing their own pension, each simply matching whatever behaviour happens to be locally normal, regardless of whether it actually suits their own circumstances.

The question worth asking before you copy

None of this means the crowd is always wrong. Sometimes the group genuinely does know something you don't, and dismissing every popular choice out of pure contrarianism is its own kind of foolishness, just running in the opposite direction. The useful skill isn't refusing to ever follow the crowd. It's learning to notice the moment you're doing it and asking one honest question before you go any further. Am I buying this because I've independently assessed it and believe it's a good decision, or am I buying it because everyone around me appears to be buying it, and that feels like evidence in itself.

If it's the second, that feeling is not new information about the investment. It's an old piece of machinery, extremely well suited to warning you about predators near a water hole, doing its level best to help you decide whether to put money into an asset it has absolutely no capacity to actually evaluate. Recognising which one is talking, your careful judgement or your monkey's ancient instinct to run because everyone else is running, is very often the entire difference between a sensible decision and an expensive one.

CHAPTER 6
TOMORROW NEVER COMES

Back in Chapter One, I introduced you to the stranger. The version of you retiring in thirty years, who your own brain treats less like a future self and more like a distant cousin you've never actually met. I won't repeat that argument here. Instead, I want to show you exactly where this shows up in the financial choices you're making this week, often several times a day, usually without noticing it's happening at all.

The four easy payments

Start with something you've almost certainly seen at a checkout, online or in person. Rather than one price, you're offered a smaller number, repeated four times, spread a few weeks apart. Buy now, split the cost, nothing due until later.

The maths hasn't changed. You're paying exactly the same total either way, in most cases without even the small mercy of interest making the split expensive enough to notice. What's changed is how the cost is presented to a brain that discounts the future steeply and the present barely at all. A single upfront figure asks you to feel the entire cost right now, in one go, at the moment your judgement is sharpest. Four smaller figures ask you to feel a quarter of it now and quietly agree to feel the rest later, at a point your present self will barely be thinking about it.

This works precisely because of the wiring covered in Chapter One. Your present self, the one standing at the checkout, cares enormously about avoiding discomfort right now. Your future self, the one who'll actually pay the second, third and fourth instalments, is that same distant stranger who barely registers as you at all. Splitting a cost into pieces doesn't reduce what you owe. It simply moves most of the discomfort onto someone your brain has already decided isn't fully your problem.

The minimum payment trap

Credit card statements offer a similar trick, and it's built more deliberately than it first appears, because the mechanics are more deliberate than they first appear.

Every statement carries two figures. The full balance, and a much smaller minimum payment, usually printed in a way that draws the eye toward the smaller number rather than the larger one. Paying only the minimum feels, in the moment, like a perfectly responsible choice. You've paid something. The account stays in good standing. Nothing bad happens today.

What doesn't register, because it belongs entirely to

a future your present self isn't especially invested in, is how long clearing the balance will actually take at that minimum figure, and how much extra you'll hand over in interest along the way. A balance that could be cleared in a matter of months, paid off properly, can stretch out over years at the minimum, quietly costing considerably more than the original amount borrowed. None of that cost is felt today. It arrives in small, barely noticeable instalments, addressed to a future self who was never going to complain about it very loudly.

This is present bias operating almost perfectly. The pain of paying more now is vivid and immediate. The pain of paying considerably more later, spread thin across years, barely registers as pain at all.

The overdraft that becomes a fact of life

There's a third version of this worth naming properly, quieter than the other two, and precisely because it's quiet, it's arguably the one that costs the most people the most money over the longest stretch of time without ever once feeling like a decision at all.

An overdraft usually starts as a genuine, temporary rescue. A bill lands a few days before payday, the account dips below zero for a short stretch, the overdraft absorbs the gap, and normal service resumes the following week. Nothing about that first use is unreasonable. It's exactly what an overdraft facility exists for. The trouble starts quietly, months or sometimes years later, when the account never quite climbs back into consistently positive territory, and being a little overdrawn simply becomes the account's permanent resting state rather than an occasional rescue.

Ask someone in this position whether they intend to clear it, and almost everyone says yes, obviously, once things ease up a bit. But clearing an overdraft requires the present self to accept a genuinely uncomfortable month, spending noticeably less than usual in order to build the balance back into positive territory, and that discomfort is due right now, vivid and immediate, in exchange for a benefit, no longer paying overdraft interest, that belongs entirely to a future self who, once again, doesn't feel quite real enough to motivate the sacrifice. So the uncomfortable month keeps getting postponed, the same way saving properly keeps getting postponed, and the overdraft interest, individually small on any given day, quietly accumulates into a genuinely significant cost over a year, then several years, without ever once presenting itself as a single, large, attention grabbing decision that might have prompted action.

This is present bias at its most invisible, precisely because there's no single moment where a clear choice gets made badly. Nobody sits down and decides to stay overdrawn for three years. The decision simply never gets made at all, month after month, each individual month's inaction feeling entirely reasonable in isolation, right up until someone finally adds up the total cost and discovers quite how much a temporary rescue quietly became a permanent and expensive habit.

• • •

Why saving for later never quite happens

Here's where the present bias story connects directly back to your own future, rather than someone else's product. Ask most people whether they intend to save more, start a pension, or build up a proper reserve, and almost everyone says yes, of course, eventually. Ask them to actually move money out of this month's account into that future right now, and the enthusiasm cools fast.

There's a particular sentence to listen for in yourself, because it comes up constantly and it's almost always a present bias tell rather than a genuine plan. I'll start saving properly once I'm earning a bit more. It sounds sensible. It sounds like patience rather than avoidance. But notice what it actually does. It doesn't commit your present self to anything today. It quietly hands the decision to a future self who, by the time that future actually arrives, will very likely be having exactly the same thought about the self one step further along again. The goalpost doesn't get reached. It gets pushed forward at roughly the same speed you're walking toward it.

There's genuine science behind why this particular delay is so stubborn, and it's worth being honest about a complication in it rather than presenting it as fully settled. Studies of delayed reward preferences in monkeys have consistently found steep discounting of anything not available immediately, mirroring the same pattern in humans reasonably closely. Some researchers argue this reflects genuine impatience, an active preference for now over later. Others have made a more technical case, that some of what looks like impatience might actually be a kind of forgetting, the value of the delayed reward simply fading from memory across the gap, rather than being actively devalued in the moment of choosing. It's an open question, and a useful one to sit with, because it suggests two rather different fixes. If it's impatience, you need to make the present cost of not saving feel real. If it's forgetting, you need to make the future reward impossible to lose sight of. Either way, waiting for motivation to arrive naturally is not, on this evidence, a strategy likely to work.

The January membership that outlasts January

One final scenario shows present bias operating at the moment of commitment itself, rather than at the moment of avoiding a decision.

A new year, or any other symbolic fresh start, prompts a burst of motivation and a membership signed up for in full, often annual, often paid upfront or committed to on a rolling monthly basis that's considerably easier to start than to later stop. In that moment, the future self, doing the exercising, eating well, finally getting fitter, feels vivid, real, and close at hand. Close enough that committing money to them feels like an easy, even exciting decision. The present self, signing the agreement isn't being asked to sacrifice anything uncomfortable right now. Quite the opposite, the signing itself feels good, a small hit of identity and possibility purchased for the price of a signature.

The trouble arrives a few weeks later, once the initial motivation has faded and the actual, repeated, mildly uncomfortable effort of showing up becomes the present reality rather than a vivid future intention. Present bias, having made signing up feel effortless, now works in exactly the opposite direction, making the ongoing cost of a membership already committed to feel easy to ignore, a small, recurring deduction rather than a decision anyone actively has to keep making. The same brain that discounted the difficulty of showing up in January discounts the wasted monthly fee just as readily in February, March, and every month after, precisely because neither the effort nor the cost ever presents itself as a single, attention grabbing moment worth acting on.

The pattern underneath all five

Look at the four easy payments, the minimum payment trap, the overdraft that quietly became permanent, the January membership, and the perpetually postponed savings plan side by side, and the same shape appears each time. A cost or a benefit sits in the future. The present self, the one actually making the decision, discounts it heavily, almost automatically, without any conscious weighing up at all. And a decision gets made that feels entirely reasonable in the moment and turns out to be expensive, or simply never happens, once that future eventually arrives and becomes the present.

None of this makes you weak willed. It makes you, once again, exactly as wired as every other primate whose discounting curve researchers have ever measured. The stranger you're supposedly protecting yourself from disappointing, next month's you, next year's you, the retired version of you decades from now, was never going to feel real enough in the moment to compete fairly against whatever felt urgent today.

What actually works against this, and we'll get to it properly in Part Four, isn't trying to summon more willpower or more concern for a future self who will always struggle to feel real. It's removing the decision from the moment entirely, so your present self never gets asked to sacrifice anything for a stranger in the first place. But that's a chapter for later. For now, it's enough to notice the pattern the next time a checkout offers to split your payment into four, or a statement quietly nudges you toward the smaller figure, or you catch yourself promising, once again, to start properly next month.

CHAPTER 7

MINE IS BETTER BECAUSE IT'S MINE

Ask someone what they'd pay to buy their own house, exactly as it stands today, if they didn't already own it, and you'll often get a lower number than what they'd insist on if you asked them to sell it. Same house. Same street. Same slightly damp cellar and slightly too small kitchen. The only thing that's changed between the two questions is which side of the transaction they're imagining themselves on.

This is the endowment effect, and it's one of the odder tricks your monkey plays on you, because unlike loss aversion or present bias, it doesn't obviously connect to any ancient survival problem at first glance. It's simply this. The moment something becomes yours, you value it more than you would if it were still sitting on a shelf, untouched, belonging to someone else. Ownership itself seems to add value that was never actually there.

. . .

Proof, again, from the monkeys

The same Yale researchers who ran the monkey marketplace went looking for this effect too, and found it. In a follow up study, capuchins who were given a food item to hold, briefly, before being offered the chance to trade it for a different item of supposedly equal value, showed a marked reluctance to trade. Once the item was in their possession, even for a short time, it had apparently become worth more to them than an identical item they didn't yet have.

This matters for the same reason the original marketplace findings mattered. It rules out the easy explanation that endowment effects in humans are somehow cultural, a learned attachment to property picked up from a society that prizes ownership. A capuchin monkey holding a piece of food for a few minutes has no concept of property law, inheritance, or status through possessions. And it still valued the thing in its hand more than the equivalent thing in someone else's hand. Whatever is driving this appears to sit somewhere very old and very basic in how a primate brain assigns value, well beneath anything you could call a cultural attitude toward ownership.

Your house, valued by someone who lives in it

The clearest, most expensive version of this in ordinary financial life is property, and it's worth being honest about how often it distorts genuinely important decisions.

Homeowners asked to estimate what their own house is worth tend, reliably, to land on a higher figure than an independent valuation would produce, sometimes by a meaningful margin. This isn't dishonesty. It's the endowment effect operating exactly as advertised. The house isn't just a structure with a market value to the person living in it. It's the kitchen where a particular argument got resolved, the garden a child learned to walk in, the door frame with pencil marks charting someone's height over a decade. None of that has the slightest bearing on what a buyer would actually pay for the property. But it gets folded into the owner's sense of what the house is worth regardless, quietly inflating the number before a single conversation with an estate agent has even happened.

This becomes a genuinely expensive problem the moment a sale is actually needed. An overpriced house sits on the market longer than it should. Price reductions, when they eventually come, feel like a loss rather than a correction, which drags decisions out further still, sometimes costing the seller more in delay, fees and eventual concessions than a realistic price from the outset ever would have. The house didn't get less valuable while sitting unsold. The owner's estimate of its value was simply never quite accurate to begin with, inflated from day one by nothing more than the fact of living there.

The portfolio you won't rebalance

A quieter, less visible version of the same trap shows up in investment portfolios, and it often masquerades as loyalty or conviction rather than what it actually is.

Investors frequently hold onto a particular stock,

fund, or investment simply because they already own it, well past the point where a genuinely fresh look would lead them to choose it again from scratch. Ask the honest question, would I buy this specific holding today, at today's price, if I were building my portfolio from nothing, and the answer is very often no. But the holding stays anyway, not because a careful analysis says it should, but because it's already there, already part of what feels like mine, and parting with it carries a whiff of loss the way selling any endowed possession does.

This shows up especially strongly with shares in a person's own employer, or investments inherited from a parent or acquired during some formative period of their financial life. The emotional weight of already owning something, particularly something tied to identity or memory, makes an honest, dispassionate reassessment considerably harder than it would be for a stranger's identical portfolio, evaluated with no history attached at all.

The business that's worth more because it's yours

Business owners, quite understandably, tend to value their own business more highly than an outside buyer or investor typically would. Years of effort, personal risk, and identity get folded into the number, in exactly the way memories get folded into a homeowner's estimate of their house. The business, purely as an asset, might be worth a certain figure to a detached buyer assessing only its future cash flows and market position. To the person who built it, sacrificed for it, and still thinks of it as something closer to a child than a spreadsheet, it's worth considerably more than that, regardless of what any buyer would actually pay.

This gap between the founder's valuation and the market's valuation is one of the most common reasons a genuinely good business fails to sell or sells for less than expected after an owner finally accepts a lower offer than the one they spent months rejecting. The business didn't change value during that standoff. The owner's estimate of it was simply never built on the same foundation a buyer's would be.

The house that took three years to clear

There's a version of the endowment effect I've watched play out with particular intensity around inheritance. It shows how the bias can attach itself to objects that were never really about money at all, and how expensive that attachment can quietly become.

A parent dies, and their house needs to be cleared and eventually sold, a task that falls to their adult children at precisely the moment they're least equipped to make clear headed decisions about anything. Every item in that house, individually near worthless in resale terms, a dinner service, a set of tools, furniture that would struggle to find a buyer at a car boot sale, carries an entirely different weight to the people going through it, because each object is endowed not just with ordinary ownership but with grief, memory and the last physical traces of a person who's gone. A worn armchair that a stranger would price at a few pounds becomes, to a grieving son or daughter, something that feels almost impossible to simply give away.

What happens next, more often than most people expect, is that the house itself sits empty for months, sometimes years, because nobody in the family can quite bring themselves to sort through it properly, and the actual sale of the property, a genuinely significant financial asset, gets delayed indefinitely behind the much smaller, much more emotionally loaded task of deciding what to do with the contents. The financial cost of this delay, an empty property accruing council tax, insurance, maintenance and lost interest on money that could have been invested elsewhere, is often considerable, and almost never weighed consciously against the emotional cost of finally letting the smaller items go. The endowment effect here isn't really about the dinner service or the armchair being worth more because they're owned. It's that they're the last physical evidence of a relationship, and parting with them feels, however irrationally, like parting with the relationship itself. Recognising that distinction, that the reluctance is genuinely about grief rather than genuinely about value, is often the thing that finally allows a family to separate the two decisions, honouring the memory in whatever way actually matters to them, while no longer holding an entire, considerably more valuable asset hostage to it.

Why this one is harder to catch than most

Loss aversion at least announces itself, a decision that involves selling at a loss tends to feel uncomfortable in a fairly recognisable way. The endowment effect is quieter and more insidious, because it doesn't feel like bias at all. It feels like an accurate assessment of genuine value, based on genuinely relevant information, my house, my portfolio, my business, that only I could possibly know about.

The test to apply, whenever a valuation feels certain purely because the thing being valued is already yours, is the same one in every case. Would I value this the same way, arrive at the same number, if it had never been mine at all, if I encountered it today for the first time as a stranger. If the honest answer is no, the gap between those two numbers isn't insight. It's a capuchin refusing to trade the food already in its hand for an identical piece sitting a few feet away, dressed up as a considered financial judgement.

Worth remembering, before moving on, that none of this makes ownership itself a mistake. A house is still a home regardless of what a stranger's valuation says. The error isn't in loving what's yours. It's in quietly letting that love masquerade as a financial figure, one you'd defend to a buyer as though it were arrived at independently, rather than one shaped, at least in part, by the simple, powerful fact of already holding it in your hand.

CHAPTER 8

KEEPING UP WITH THE TROOP

Okay, you may already have seen the clip. One of my very favourites. It's also one of the most shared pieces of animal footage online, which is usually a sign that a study has been flattened into a punchline on the way to going viral. This one hasn't been. It's also one of the more carefully designed experiments in this book, and the debate it kicked off is still running. It's a video of a capuchin monkey handed a piece of cucumber as a reward for completing a simple task. She eats it happily enough, until she watches the monkey in the next enclosure complete the exact same task and receive a grape instead. Grapes, to a capuchin, are considerably more exciting than cucumber. The first monkey looks at her cucumber, looks at the other monkey's grape, and, quite unmistakably, loses her mind. She flings the cucumber back at the researcher and rattles the enclosure in what can only be described as pure indignation and rage.

This is one of the most cited findings in behavioural science, and it deserves to be, because it reveals something about value that most of us intuitively know and almost never admit out loud. The cucumber didn't change. It was perfectly good food a moment earlier. What changed was entirely relative, purely a matter of what someone else nearby had just received for doing the identical job.

What the grape study actually found

The researchers behind this, Sarah Brosnan and Frans de Waal, ran the experiment properly rather than just filming a viral clip. Capuchin monkeys were trained to trade a token for a food reward. When both monkeys in a pair received the same reward for the same effort, cucumber for both or grape for both, trading continued smoothly. The moment one monkey started receiving grapes while its partner kept receiving cucumber, the cucumber recipient's cooperation collapsed. Monkeys who had been perfectly satisfied with cucumber right up until they saw a neighbour get grapes suddenly refused to participate at all, some refusing to even eat the cucumber they'd previously happily accepted.

It's worth being straightforward about the fact that not every researcher agrees on exactly what this proves. A response published shortly afterward argued the monkeys' reaction might be better explained as simple frustration at seeing a better reward nearby and not receiving it, a kind of contrast effect, rather than genuine reasoning about fairness between two parties.

Brosnan and de Waal published a reply defending the original interpretation, and the debate has continued in various forms since. What's not in dispute, whichever explanation turns out to be correct, is the underlying behavioural fact itself. A reward that was entirely satisfactory in isolation becomes unsatisfactory the moment a comparable reward appears to go to someone else. Whether you call that a sense of fairness or simply a sharp, involuntary reaction to relative disadvantage, the practical result on your own financial decisions turns out to be exactly the same either way.

Why your own perfectly good car suddenly feels inadequate

Here's where the cucumber and the grape stop being a story about monkeys and start being a story about your driveway.

You bought a car at some point because it suited your needs, sat comfortably within your budget, and did the job you needed it to do. Nothing about that car changes when a neighbour buys a newer one. The engine performs identically. The commute takes exactly as long. And yet something genuinely does shift, an itch that wasn't there the week before, a faint but real sense that your own choice, perfectly satisfactory a fortnight ago, has quietly become the cucumber.

This is lifestyle creep in its purest form, and it rarely announces itself as comparison. It shows up dressed as a reasonable, independent desire to upgrade, timed suspiciously often to coincide with someone else's new purchase. The car, the kitchen renovation, the holiday destination, the size of a wedding, all of it gets evaluated not purely on its own merits but against a constantly shifting local benchmark set by whoever happens to be nearby. Move house to a wealthier street and, with no change whatsoever to your own income or needs, the benchmark quietly resets upward, and possessions that felt more than adequate the month before start to feel oddly insufficient.

Researchers studying life satisfaction and income have found this pattern reliably across large populations, not just in anecdote. People's reported satisfaction with their own income depends heavily on how it compares with those around them, sometimes more heavily than it depends on the actual amount itself. A raise that moves you ahead of your peer group can feel genuinely satisfying even if your real purchasing power barely shifts. An identical raise that leaves you still behind your peer group can feel disappointing even though, in absolute terms, you're better off than you were before. The number in your account matters. The number next door appears, for a great many people, to matter almost as much.

The wedding that grew by a third

Weddings deserve a mention of their own, because they show the comparison instinct operating at unusually high stakes, over an unusually short and emotionally loaded window, in a way that makes the underlying mechanism easier to see than almost anywhere else.

A couple planning a wedding typically start with a

genuinely sensible figure in mind, based honestly on what they can comfortably afford. Then the planning begins in earnest, and with it, a steady stream of comparisons neither partner necessarily set out to make. A friend's wedding last summer had a particular kind of venue, and suddenly the venue under consideration feels slightly less impressive by comparison, regardless of whether it was ever meant to compete with anyone else's day. A sibling's wedding had a live band, and a decision that once felt entirely optional starts to feel, quite irrationally, like a bare minimum rather than a genuine choice. None of these comparisons get made consciously or maliciously. They arrive quietly, the same way the neighbour's new car quietly makes your own feel inadequate, one grape at a time, each individually reasonable, collectively pushing a carefully considered original budget considerably higher than either partner ever intended.

The number that actually lands, for a great many couples, ends up meaningfully larger than the number they started with, not because their actual wants changed, but because the local benchmark set by recently attended weddings kept quietly resetting upward throughout the planning process. Ask either partner afterward whether any single addition, in isolation, was unreasonable, and the honest answer is usually no. Ask whether the final total, added up and looked at cold, is what they'd have chosen if no comparable wedding had ever crossed their path first, and the honest answer is very often, just as clearly, also no.

Salary, status and the number that was never really about the money

This same mechanism explains a pattern that puzzles a lot of people about their own reactions to pay. Ask someone whether they'd rather earn a certain amount while everyone around them earns more, or earn somewhat less while everyone around them earns even less again, and a striking number choose the second option, actively preferring less money in absolute terms provided it comes with a favourable comparison. Purely rational self interest, judged only by what that money can actually buy, says this makes no sense whatsoever. The grape and cucumber study suggests it makes a great deal of sense to a brain that evolved in small groups where relative standing genuinely did determine access to mates, allies and resources, long before absolute wealth in any modern sense existed as a concept at all.

This has real financial consequences beyond simple envy. Negotiating pay, choosing a job, deciding whether a role feels fairly rewarded, all of it gets quietly filtered through comparison with colleagues, friends and a curated, highlight reel version of strangers on social media, rather than through any honest assessment of whether the number itself meets your actual needs and goals. The comparison isn't irrelevant information exactly. But it is very often given far more weight in a financial decision than it actually deserves, purely because a brain built for a forty person group finds relative standing almost impossible to ignore.

The version amplified by a screen

There's one modern complication the capuchins never had to contend with; social media. Social comparison used to be bounded by geography and circumstance, limited to whoever actually lived nearby or worked alongside you. A phone now puts a curated, near constant stream of other people's holidays, renovations and purchases in front of you dozens of times a day, almost none of it an honest or representative picture of those people's actual finances. The comparison instinct hasn't changed since the days of a forty person troop. The volume and selectiveness of what it's being fed most certainly has, and this almost certainly makes the whole effect considerably harder to manage than it would have been for a monkey whose entire comparison group lived within shouting distance.

Cucumber is still perfectly good cucumber

None of this means comparison is inherently irrational or that you should somehow train yourself to stop noticing what other people have, which isn't a realistic goal for a primate brain built exactly the way yours is. One plain fact is worth remembering every time an upgrade starts to feel suddenly urgent for no clear reason of your own. The cucumber didn't get worse. It's still exactly the food it always was, still doing the job it was always going to do. What changed was only ever the grape next door, and the grape next door has no actual bearing whatsoever on whether your own choice was, and still is, a perfectly good one.

Picture the capuchin from the start of this chapter

one more time, cucumber in hand, glancing sideways at her neighbour's grape. Nobody took anything away from her. Nobody changed the terms of her own deal. The cucumber sitting in her hand a moment before the grape appeared was, by every honest measure, exactly as satisfying as it had been the moment before. The only thing that moved was her attention, drawn sideways toward a comparison that had nothing to do with her own circumstances at all. The next time an upgrade starts to feel urgent, ask plainly whether anything about your own situation has actually changed, or whether you've simply caught sight of somebody else's grape.

CHAPTER 9

NO MONKEY TO BE SEEN

I've spent eight chapters introducing you to a monkey and asking you to forgive yourself a little more generously for the things he gets up to. This chapter is different, and deliberately so. It's the one place in this book where I'm going to look you in the eye and say, no, that one isn't him. That one's on you.

The bias that wasn't there

The same Yale researchers who found loss aversion and the endowment effect in capuchin monkeys went looking for a third bias too, one that shows up constantly in human shopping and negotiating. Anchoring, the tendency for an arbitrary number, a first price mentioned, a figure glimpsed moments earlier, to quietly shape what you're willing to pay for something afterward, even when that number has no genuine connection to the item's actual worth.

Anchoring in humans is remarkably well documented and remarkably easy to demonstrate. Show someone a high number immediately before asking them to estimate the value of something entirely unrelated, and their estimate drifts upward. Show them a low number instead, and it drifts downward. The number doesn't need to make sense. Studies have produced this effect using numbers as arbitrary as the last two digits of someone's own phone number. It shouldn't work. It reliably does.

So the researchers ran the equivalent test on their capuchins, giving them an arbitrary price signal before a trading decision, the exact kind of manipulation that reliably shifts human behaviour. And the monkeys simply weren't affected. Their trading stayed consistent with the item's actual value to them, unmoved by whatever arbitrary number had been shown beforehand. The same population that had shown loss aversion, that had shown the endowment effect, both wired in deeply enough to survive with no cultural transmission whatsoever, showed absolutely nothing here.

The researchers themselves drew the conclusion plainly. Anchoring, unlike the other biases in this book, may depend on cognitive machinery that's uniquely human. Something to do, most likely, with our particular gift and curse for language, for holding an arbitrary number in working memory and letting it silently anchor a completely separate judgement made moments later. Whatever the exact mechanism, the practical point for you is this. There is no ancient monkey wiring making you fall for an anchored price.

That particular vulnerability appears to be something we built entirely ourselves.

Where anchoring actually shows up

You'll recognise it the moment it's named properly. A house listed at a price clearly above what any comparable property nearby would fetch, which then makes a modest reduction feel, quite irrationally, like a genuine bargain rather than simply a smaller overcharge. A negotiation where whoever states a number first, almost regardless of how reasonable that number actually is, quietly sets the entire range the rest of the conversation unfolds within. A sale advertised as reduced from a higher original price, a price that may never have actually applied to very many customers at all, which nonetheless makes the current price feel like a genuine saving rather than simply the price.

None of this works because your ancient wiring is being exploited. It works because you, specifically as a modern human with language and working memory, are vulnerable to a number sitting in your head shaping a judgement you make moments later, in a way a capuchin monkey with no capacity for that kind of abstract number holding simply isn't. Recognising anchoring doesn't require forgiving yourself for ancient instincts. It requires the much more mundane and considerably more actionable discipline of ignoring the number you were shown first and independently working out what something is actually worth to you, from scratch, every single time.

It's worth seeing this play out in a single, concrete

moment, because the effect is genuinely stronger than most people expect until they've watched it happen to themselves. Picture a salary negotiation where you're asked, fairly early in the conversation, what figure you currently earn, or what you'd expect for the role. Whatever number leaves your mouth first, reasonable or not, tends to become the quiet centre of gravity for everything that follows, the employer's counter offer calculated as some adjustment from your figure rather than built independently from what the role is genuinely worth to them. Name a number too low, out of caution or a wish to seem reasonable, and the entire negotiation tends to settle lower than it otherwise would have, not because the employer deliberately exploited your caution, but because your own opening figure became the anchor the rest of the conversation quietly measured itself against. A capuchin monkey has never once experienced this, because a capuchin monkey has no language with which to be asked the question, and no working memory mechanism that would let an early number silently reshape a judgement made minutes later. This particular vulnerability belongs entirely to you, as a modern, talking, remembering human, and to nobody else in the animal kingdom your book has spent nine chapters getting to know.

The gap that has nothing to do with wiring at all

There's a second, larger category worth being equally honest about here, and it's one that runs right through everything covered so far in this book without ever being named directly. Not every financial mistake is a bias at all. A great many are simply gaps in knowledge, and no amount of understanding your inner monkey will close them.

Not knowing what compound interest actually does to a debt over years, rather than just knowing the phrase. Not understanding what a fee expressed as a small annual percentage actually costs, in real terms, compounded across several decades of investing. Not knowing the genuine difference between one type of savings product and another, or what a piece of jargon on a form actually commits you to. These aren't failures of instinct. They're failures of information, often because nobody ever sat down and explained the mechanics clearly, in plain language, at the point where it would have actually mattered.

Take the compound interest example properly, rather than just naming it, because here's how large this particular gap can be. Most people, asked casually, know that debt left unpaid accrues interest, and could probably recite the definition of compound interest if pushed. Considerably fewer people, asked to actually estimate what a moderate debt left entirely unpaid would grow into after a decade, land anywhere close to the real figure, because the mechanics of compounding produce a curve that gets steeper the longer it runs, in a way flat, straight line intuition simply doesn't anticipate. This isn't a bias in the sense the rest of this book has used the word. A capuchin monkey has no compound interest to misjudge, because compound interest doesn't exist anywhere in nature for a wild animal to have evolved an intuition about, correct or otherwise. It's a purely human financial invention, and understanding it properly is a purely human skill nobody is born with. You either learn it, properly, at some point, or you don't, and if you don't, no amount of insight into ancient wiring will help you at all.

This distinction matters more than it might first appear, because the fix for each is completely different. A bias, the kind covered in the previous eight chapters, needs a system built around it, something we'll get to properly in Part Four, because knowing about loss aversion doesn't stop you feeling it in the moment any more than knowing about optical illusions stops you seeing them. A genuine knowledge gap needs something far simpler. Just the knowledge itself, explained once, properly, in a way that actually sticks.

A second worked example, closer to my own financial services background, is worth including because it shows how a knowledge gap can persist for years even among people who consider themselves reasonably financially literate. Ask most people to explain the practical difference between a handful of common savings and investment product types, precisely what each one actually does, what happens to the money inside it, what the tax treatment genuinely means for them personally, and the honest answers are often vague, sometimes confidently wrong, occasionally entirely absent. This isn't unique to any one country's products. Every financial system develops its own thicket of product names, acronyms and rules, each one entirely sensible to the person who designed it, none of it particularly intuitive to the person expected to choose correctly between them without any formal training. A monkey never has to choose between two structurally different savings products with genuinely different tax consequences. You do, repeatedly, throughout your adult life, and nobody ever quite finds the right moment to sit you down and properly explain the difference.

Why this chapter matters for everything that follows

I've put this chapter here deliberately, at the exact midpoint of the book, because it protects the honesty of everything around it. If every single financial mistake in this book got blamed on ancient wiring, you'd have every right to be suspicious of the whole argument, and rightly so. A book that explains away every bad decision as biology isn't offering insight. It's offering an excuse dressed up as science.

So here's the line, drawn as clearly as I can draw it. Where a behaviour shows up reliably in monkeys who've never seen a bank statement, who've never been taught a single financial concept, who are separated from you by tens of millions of years of evolution, that's your monkey talking, and the fair response is understanding rather than self criticism. Where a behaviour depends on something uniquely human, like anchoring, or simply on information nobody ever properly explained to you, that's a different problem entirely, one that deserves a different kind of honesty and a different kind of fix.

This distinction is about to matter for a different reason too, one we'll pick up properly in the next part of this book. Because it turns out the people designing the products and adverts you encounter every day aren't only working with your ancient wiring. They're often working with exactly these same uniquely human vulnerabilities too, the arbitrary anchors, the confusing small print, the gaps in understanding that never quite get closed. Not because anyone behind the counter is plotting against you. But because, as we're about to see, they're frequently just as wired, and just as human, as you are.

CHAPTER 10
THE MONKEYS ON THE OTHER SIDE OF THE COUNTER

You've now spent nine chapters getting to know your own monkey, in reasonable detail, across most of the situations where he actually costs you money. It's time to turn around and look at the other side of the counter, because there's a monkey standing there too, and understanding him or her properly changes how you see almost everything this part of the book is about to cover.

Nobody designed this on purpose

Here's the assumption worth dismantling early, because it's tempting and it's wrong. It's easy to imagine the financial products you encounter every day as the output of a small group of people sitting in a room, deliberately mapping out human weaknesses and building traps to exploit them one by one. That version makes for a satisfying villain. It's also, almost always, not what actually happened.

What actually happens is considerably less dramatic

and, in its own way, considerably more interesting. A product gets built. A piece of marketing gets written. A statement gets designed with one figure larger than another. Somebody tests a few versions against real customer behaviour, because that's simply how modern product design works, and one version performs better than the others. Nobody in that meeting necessarily used the words loss aversion or present bias. They just noticed, the way a market trader notices which fruit sells faster stacked a certain way, that this version converts better than that one. The better performing version gets kept. The other gets quietly dropped. Repeat that process enough times, across enough products, over enough years, and you end up with an entire industry whose designs fit the shape of the human mind with startling precision, without a single person ever having set out to study that mind deliberately.

I've sat in the room for a version of this meeting more times than I could count. Nobody arrives with a villain's brief. They arrive with a dashboard, a deadline, and a version B that's converting eleven per cent better than version A. What I've watched isn't a conspiracy. It's a feedback loop, running quietly in the background of thousands of ordinary business decisions, each one entirely reasonable in isolation, each one nudging the industry's designs a little further toward whatever the monkey brain on the other end of the screen happens to respond to most readily.

How a feedback loop actually runs, in practice

Here's a plausible version of exactly how this

unfolds, because the abstract description undersells how ordinary, even boring, each individual step genuinely is.

A product team is redesigning a customer statement, deciding how to lay out two figures, a full balance and a smaller minimum amount due. Nobody in the room sets out to exploit anyone. The genuine goal, stated plainly in the meeting, is simply making the statement clearer and easier to act on. Two versions get built, one where both figures appear the same size, one where the minimum amount is made visually larger, easier to spot at a glance. Both versions get tested against real customers, because that's standard practice, an entirely uncontroversial step nobody would think twice about. The version with the larger minimum figure produces a measurably higher proportion of customers making a payment of some kind rather than none at all, which looks, quite reasonably, like a genuine improvement. Fewer missed payments. Better customer outcomes, on the specific measure the team was actually tracking. The larger minimum figure design gets adopted.

Nobody in that room needed to have read a word about loss aversion or present bias to reach that decision. They were simply optimising for a perfectly legitimate goal, more customers making some payment rather than none, using perfectly standard testing methods, and the version that won happened to be the version that spoke most directly to a present biased brain looking for the smallest, easiest, least effortful action available. A year later, another team, at another company, redesigning their own statement, looks at what the wider industry does, notices the larger minimum figure has become close to standard practice, and adopts a similar approach themselves, reasonably assuming an established convention must reflect something sensible. The design spreads, refined and reinforced at every step by real customer data, without a single person along the way needing any knowledge of the psychology it happens to be built on.

A second monkey, not a villain

This is where the phrase in this chapter's title earns its place. The people building these products are not a different species from you. They have their own present bias, nudging a project toward whatever ships fastest and performs best this quarter, rather than whatever would genuinely serve a customer best over thirty years. They have their own herding instinct, copying whatever competitors are already doing successfully, on the reasonable assumption that if it's working for everyone else, it's probably worth doing too. They have their own loss aversion, making it considerably easier to keep a design that's already converting well than to risk changing it for something untested, even if the untested version might genuinely serve customers better.

In other words, the industry isn't run by people immune to everything covered in Part Two of this book. It's largely run by people every bit as wired as you are, applying their own instincts to the problem of building something that performs, and discovering, entirely honestly, that the designs which perform best are very often the ones that speak most directly to instincts they've never had to name or study to exploit effectively.

This matters enormously for how you read the rest of Part Three. Every example in the next two chapters could be told as a story about deliberate manipulation, and in a small number of genuinely bad actors, that story would even be true. But for the great majority of what you'll recognise in your own financial life, a more honest and considerably more useful story is available. Nobody needed to be a villain. A feedback loop, running for years, quietly did the rest.

Why regulation keeps arriving, and keeps being needed

Here's a detail that offers genuine, independent evidence for the feedback loop argument rather than asking you to simply take my word for it. Financial regulation, across most developed markets, keeps arriving in waves, each wave specifically targeting some design or practice that's become widespread enough to cause genuine, measurable harm at scale. Rules requiring clearer statement layouts. Rules requiring cooling off periods on certain products. Rules requiring fees to be expressed in ways ordinary customers can actually understand and compare.

If the industry were simply full of individually malicious actors, you'd expect regulation to arrive once, target the villains directly, and largely finish the job. What actually happens looks rather different, and rather more consistent with the feedback loop story than the villain story. A design pattern emerges gradually, through the entirely unremarkable process covered earlier in this chapter, spreads across the industry precisely because it performs well, and only once it's become genuinely widespread, adopted independently by many different firms who each arrived at something similar through their own separate testing, does the pattern become visible enough, and harmful enough in aggregate, for a regulator to notice and act on it. This is exactly what a feedback loop looks like from the outside, a pattern nobody centrally designed nonetheless spreading and repeating until it becomes large enough to require a deliberate, external correction. Recent obligations requiring firms to evidence that their products genuinely deliver fair value to customers exist precisely because the ordinary, undirected process of design and testing doesn't reliably produce fair outcomes on its own, not because an industry of villains needed catching, but because a feedback loop, left entirely to itself, drifts toward whatever converts, and fair value was never guaranteed to be the same thing as what converts best.

Why the distinction actually matters to you

You might reasonably ask why this distinction matters at all, given that the effect on your wallet is identical either way. A product shaped by careful, deliberate exploitation costs you exactly as much as an identical product shaped by an accidental feedback loop nobody fully understood while building it.

It matters for one practical reason above all others. If

you go looking for villains, you'll only spot the products that feel deliberately sinister, the ones with genuinely predatory intent behind them, and you'll miss almost everything else, because most of what shapes your financial decisions every day was never built with intent to harm you at all. It was simply built to convert, tested against real behaviour, and kept because it worked. That's a far larger and far more common category than deliberate villainy, and if you're only trained to spot the villains, the much bigger, quieter category will walk straight past you every single time.

The useful skill for the rest of this part of the book isn't learning to spot bad actors, although you'll certainly recognise a few. It's learning to recognise the shape of a design that fits your wiring a little too neatly, regardless of whether anyone behind it meant it that way, and asking the one question that actually protects you either way. Does this suit me, judged on its own honest merits, or does it simply suit the version of me that struggles with loss aversion, present bias, and every other instinct we've spent the last nine chapters getting to know.

What's coming

Over the next two chapters, we'll walk through exactly how this feedback loop has shaped some of the most ordinary financial products and marketing techniques you encounter regularly, from packaged accounts and fund fees to the four easy payments and the fear framed insurance add-on. None of it will require you to imagine a room full of people plotting against you. All of it will require you to recognise, clearly and specifically, when a design happens to fit your monkey a little too well, and to make your own honest decision about it anyway.

CHAPTER 11
THE ANATOMY OF AN EASY YES

Picture the modest monthly fee sitting on your bank statement, the one that bundles in travel insurance, phone cover and breakdown assistance. Nobody sat you down and sold it to you exactly. You probably just said yes. This chapter asks why saying yes felt so easy, walking through a handful of ordinary financial products and looking closely at exactly which instinct each one happens to fit so neatly, and how it most likely got that way.

The account that comes with everything

Packaged bank accounts, the kind charging a modest monthly fee in exchange for a bundle of extras, travel insurance, mobile phone cover, breakdown assistance, are a genuinely useful case study, because the appeal is entirely real and the value very often isn't.

Bundling works on a simple, well tested piece of psychology. A single monthly fee feels smaller and more manageable than the sum of what each individual benefit would cost bought separately, even when the bundle actually costs more overall than most customers would spend buying only what they need. It also plays neatly into present bias. Committing to a monthly fee now, in exchange for cover you might use at some unspecified point later, asks far less of your present self than working out, product by product, whether you'd actually buy travel insurance and phone cover and breakdown assistance individually if each carried its own separate decision and its own separate price tag.

Nobody necessarily set out to build a product depending on customers not doing that maths. Bundling tested well because bundling generally does, across almost every industry that's ever tried it, precisely because it reduces the number of decisions a present biased brain has to make. The account got kept and refined because it converted, and it converted because it fit the shape of present bias neatly, regardless of whether the value stacked up for any individual customer who actually sat down and checked.

The practical fix here has nothing to do with suspicion or villains. It's simply doing the unbundling arithmetic yourself, once, honestly. Would you buy each included benefit separately, at its standalone price, if it were offered to you as its own decision. If the honest answer for most of the bundle is no, the packaged account isn't saving you money. It's simply saving you the discomfort of making several small decisions instead of one easy one.

. . .

The fund fee dressed as skill

Active fund management, where an investor pays a noticeably higher ongoing fee in exchange for a fund manager attempting to beat the wider market, rather than simply tracking it, is a slightly different case, and worth handling carefully, because skilled active management genuinely does exist. The issue isn't that active funds are inherently a poor choice. It's how the fee tends to get framed, and which instinct that framing speaks to.

A fee expressed as a small annual percentage, one or two per cent, sounds almost too small to matter, easy to wave past in a document nobody particularly enjoys reading closely. What that framing obscures, entirely legitimately rather than deceptively in most cases, is what a seemingly small annual percentage actually compounds into over several decades of investing, often amounting to a genuinely significant portion of an investor's eventual total return. This isn't hidden information exactly. It's disclosed, usually clearly, in the relevant documentation. But disclosure and genuine understanding are two very different things, and a small percentage figure simply doesn't feel the way its multi decade compounded cost actually feels, because your brain, as covered back in Chapter One, was never built to intuitively project small numbers forward across that kind of timeframe.

Fund groups didn't necessarily design the percentage framing to obscure this. Percentage fees are simply the industry standard, easy to compare fund to fund, and genuinely reasonable as a unit of measurement in isolation. But a framing that happens to obscure long term cost, however innocently arrived at, tends to survive and spread for exactly the same feedback loop reasons covered in the last chapter. It doesn't provoke the objection a starker framing might, so it never gets tested against something more transparent, and it quietly becomes the industry norm everyone simply accepts as how fees are shown.

The extended warranty, revisited properly

We touched on extended warranties back in Chapter Three, through the lens of loss aversion specifically. Worth returning to them here through a slightly different lens, the lens of where the offer actually gets made.

The warranty is almost never offered as a cold, standalone decision, weeks after the original purchase, once the initial excitement has faded and a more measured judgement might apply. It's offered at the till, moments after you've already committed to buying the item itself, while the pleasant momentum of that decision is still fresh and a small additional yes feels like a natural continuation rather than a fresh decision requiring its own scrutiny. This isn't necessarily calculated manipulation on any individual till operator's part. It's simply where the conversion rate happens to be highest, discovered the same way almost everything else in this chapter was discovered, through years of testing what works and quietly keeping it.

. . .

The introductory rate that quietly expires

One further case study targets a slightly different instinct from the other three, and almost everyone reading this has encountered a version of it at some point without necessarily noticing the mechanism at work.

Savings accounts, mortgages and credit products are very often advertised around a headline introductory rate, genuinely attractive for a fixed initial period, that then reverts to a considerably less competitive rate once the introductory window closes. The headline figure is real, and the product genuinely does pay or charge that rate for the stated period. What tends to go unnoticed, quietly rather than deceptively in most cases, is exactly when the switch happens and what the account defaults to afterward, because very few customers actively track their own account's anniversary date the way they tracked the enticing rate when they first opened it.

This design didn't need to be built around forgetfulness deliberately. It simply survived because it worked. A genuinely attractive headline rate draws in more customers than a flat, unremarkable one, tested and confirmed the same way every other design in this chapter was confirmed. And once a customer has opened the account, present bias, the same mechanism covered fully in Chapter Six, quietly does the rest. Actively reviewing and switching an account requires effort and attention right now, in exchange for a saving that only accrues gradually, later, to a future self who was never quite motivated enough to bother. The account that once looked like the best deal on the market drifts, unnoticed, into being one of the worst, and stays there for years, not because anyone built a trap, but because inertia, once triggered, requires no further design at all to keep working in the provider's favour.

The product that promises to protect you from loss

A final case study, worth including because it sits close to the platform work I've spent most of my career around, and because it shows the feedback loop operating on genuinely sophisticated, well intentioned financial engineering rather than anything simple or obviously questionable.

Structured investment products, often marketed around some version of capital protection or a guaranteed minimum return, are built to appeal directly to loss aversion, the very first bias covered in this book. The pitch is genuinely attractive on its own terms. Participate in some of the market's potential upside, while a specific, contractually guaranteed floor protects you from the worst of any downside. For an investor who's read Chapter Three and recognises exactly how much a loss hurts compared to an equivalent gain, this can sound like precisely the right answer, a way of having the growth without quite so much of the fear.

What tends to go considerably less examined, buried in genuinely complex legal documentation that very few investors, or for that matter maybe very few of the people selling the product, read in full, is exactly how the protection is funded. It's rarely free. The upside participation is very often capped considerably below what a simple, low cost tracker fund would have delivered over the same period, and the guarantee itself frequently depends on the product being held to its full term, sometimes many years, with early withdrawal carrying costs that erase much of the protection's apparent value. None of this necessarily makes the product a bad one in every circumstance. It makes it a product built, quite understandably, around exactly the instinct most likely to make an investor say yes without working through every clause, and refined over years precisely because loss averse investors reliably find the headline pitch persuasive, whether or not they ever fully price in what the protection actually costs them in foregone growth.

What all five have in common

Look back across the packaged account, the fund fee framing, the till side warranty offer, the introductory rate that quietly expires, and the structured product built around loss aversion, and the same underlying pattern shows up each time. None of it required a single person to sit down and deliberately study loss aversion, present bias, or any other concept from Part Two of this book. Each design simply survived because it worked, tested against real customer behaviour and feedback rather than built from a psychology textbook, and kept because keeping it was the entirely rational business decision once the numbers came back.

That's precisely why the fix can't be suspicion alone.

Suspicion only catches the products that feel obviously engineered, and misses the much larger category that arrived at exactly the same place by an entirely unremarkable, entirely explicable route. The genuinely useful habit, and the one to carry into every purchase from here on, is the same simple question in every case. Strip away how easy this decision was made to feel, and ask what you'd actually choose if the exact same option were put to you cold, with no bundling, no momentum, and no percentage sign quietly doing the heavy lifting on your behalf.

CHAPTER 12

MARKETING TO THE MONKEY

"Offer ends tonight." You've seen the phrase a thousand times, blinking gently at the top of a checkout page, and some small part of you still responds to it every time, even though you know many of these deadlines aren't real. This chapter turns to marketing itself, the language and imagery wrapped around the products from the last two chapters, because marketing has its own version of exactly the same story.

The urgency that was never really about time

Almost every promotion you've ever seen carries some version of a deadline attached to it. Ends soon. Limited availability. Offer closes at midnight. The specific wording varies, but the underlying mechanism is identical every time, and it speaks directly to something covered back in Chapter Six.

A decision with no deadline invites your slower,

more deliberate thinking to get involved, the kind capable of pausing, comparing, and walking away to sleep on it. A decision with an artificial deadline attached collapses that entire process into something closer to instinct, because your present biased brain treats an imminent deadline as urgent in exactly the way it evolved to treat an immediate physical threat, regardless of whether the underlying decision has any genuine time pressure attached to it at all. Very often, quietly, the same or a similar offer reappears again a few weeks later, revealing the original deadline for what it usually was, a way of borrowing urgency your rational brain would never have volunteered on its own.

This wasn't necessarily built by someone who'd read a psychology textbook on present bias. Urgency framing simply converts better than open ended framing, tested and confirmed across countless promotions long before anyone bothered asking exactly why.

The four easy payments, seen from this side

We covered the mechanics of buy now, split later financing back in Chapter Six, so I won't repeat the psychology here. Worth noting instead, briefly, how the marketing language itself does extra work beyond the splitting mechanism alone. Easy is doing a great deal of quiet labour in that phrase. Not cheaper, not smaller, simply easy, a word aimed squarely at reducing the felt effort of a decision rather than making any claim whatsoever about its actual cost. It's a small choice of word, and it wasn't accidental. It was tested, alongside dozens of alternatives, and kept because it performed.

Fear, framed just vividly enough

Insurance marketing leans heavily on a technique worth naming plainly, because once you've seen it you'll recognise it everywhere. The specific, vivid, easily imagined bad outcome, a cracked phone screen, a burst pipe, a holiday cut short by illness, gets placed front and centre, while the actual statistical likelihood of that particular outcome, usually genuinely quite low, stays comfortably out of view.

This connects directly back to Chapter Three. Loss aversion responds to vividness, not to probability, and marketing that leads with a specific, imaginable scenario is speaking precisely that language, whether or not anyone involved in writing the copy could name loss aversion if you asked them directly. A single memorable image of disaster does more persuasive work than an accurate statistic ever could, because your monkey was never built to feel a percentage the way he or she feels a picture.

Reduced from, and the anchor that was never really there

We covered genuine anchoring properly in Chapter Nine, including the honest finding that it appears to be a uniquely human vulnerability rather than something written into ancient wiring. Marketing built around a reduced from price is one of anchoring's most common and most effective applications, and it's worth a brief mention here precisely because Chapter Nine already told you why it works so reliably. There's no ancient excuse available for falling for this one. The original, higher figure, whether or not it ever genuinely applied to meaningful numbers of customers, sits in your head for a moment and quietly reshapes what the current price feels like by comparison, exploiting a piece of cognitive machinery that belongs to you specifically as a modern, language using human, not to any monkey ancestor at all.

The number of other people already doing it

A technique that speaks directly to Chapter Five rather than to loss aversion or anchoring, is the small printed statistic that quietly accompanies a great many financial products and adverts. Over a certain number of customers switched last year. Rated highly by a certain number of reviewers. Chosen by a stated proportion of people in your situation.

These figures never make any direct claim about whether the product actually suits you personally. What they do instead, reliably and effectively, is speak straight to the herding instinct covered fully in Chapter Five, offering exactly the kind of social proof a copying brain evolved to treat as trustworthy evidence, a large number of other people apparently having already made this same choice and, by implication, found it a good one. The statistic is very often entirely accurate. It's simply irrelevant to the specific question of whether the product suits your own circumstances, and it was never included to answer that question in the first place. It was included, tested, and kept, because a headline social proof figure reliably improves how a product performs, in exactly the way a queue on the pavement outside a house viewing reliably raises the offers that follow it.

The free trial that quietly becomes a subscription

One final technique draws on more than one instinct from Part Two at once. A free trial period, genuinely free, genuinely no obligation for its stated length, that automatically converts into a paid subscription unless actively cancelled before the deadline.

The offer itself is entirely honest, stated clearly in the terms, and the free period genuinely is free. What makes this particular design so effective is how neatly it stacks two separate instincts on top of each other. Present bias, covered in Chapter Six, makes signing up today, for something genuinely free right now, an easy decision, while the cost of remembering to cancel, and the modest effort of actually doing so, both sit safely in a future that doesn't feel especially real yet. And once the trial has begun, the endowment effect from Chapter Seven starts quietly working in the provider's favour too, because a service you've already been using for a few weeks, however casually, starts to feel a little more like something you already own, making the decision to cancel feel marginally more like a loss than it would have felt as a cold, hypothetical choice before the trial ever began. Neither instinct needed to be deliberately combined by design. Both simply happened to point the same direction, and a design that happens to align two separate biases at once converts better than one that only speaks to a single instinct, which is reason enough for it to have survived and spread.

The points you'd hate to lose

Loyalty schemes, points programmes and tiered membership levels deserve a mention here too, because they speak directly to the sunk cost pattern covered fully in Chapter Four, in a form that shows up so often it's easy to stop noticing it's there at all.

Once you've accumulated a meaningful number of points, or climbed partway toward a higher membership tier, switching to a competitor stops feeling like a neutral choice between two similar options and starts feeling like abandoning something you've already built. The points themselves are very often worth considerably less, in genuine cash terms, than the effort and loyalty spent earning them, and a fresh, honest comparison between providers would frequently favour switching. But the accumulated points function exactly like the renovation from Chapter Four or the badly performing fund held out of loyalty, a sunk cost that exerts a pull on the decision entirely disproportionate to its actual remaining value. This design didn't need to be built by someone deliberately targeting the sunk cost fallacy. Loyalty schemes simply retain customers more effectively than schemes without them, tested and confirmed across countless industries, and a scheme that quietly makes switching feel like a loss will always outperform one that doesn't, regardless of whether anyone building it ever needed to name the psychology doing the work.

Why none of this requires a villain, one last time

Every technique in this chapter could be described as manipulative, and in the hands of a genuinely bad actor, some of it certainly is. But the honest, more useful reading, consistent with everything covered in this part of the book, is that almost all of it arrived at its current form the same way the products themselves did. Tested. Refined. Kept because it worked. Because the feedback was positive. Nobody necessarily needed to understand loss aversion, present bias, herding, the endowment effect, sunk cost, or anchoring by name in order to build marketing that speaks fluently to all six. They simply needed to try enough versions and keep whatever converted best, and the versions that converted best turned out, unsurprisingly, to be the ones that spoke most directly to instincts every human being on the planet already carries.

Closing Part Three

You now know your own monkey reasonably well, from Part Two, and you've spent this part of the book meeting his counterpart on the other side of the counter, not a villain exactly, simply another wired brain, building and marketing things that happen to fit the shape of everyone else's wiring rather neatly, because that's what tends to survive.

None of this knowledge makes either monkey disappear. Understanding a deadline is probably artificial doesn't stop it feeling urgent in the moment. Understanding a reduced price is anchored doesn't stop the anchor from quietly doing its work. That's precisely the limit of insight alone, and it's exactly why the rest of this book, Part Four, isn't about trying harder to notice these things in real time. It's about building systems that don't require you to notice them at all.

CHAPTER 13

SYSTEMS BEAT WILLPOWER

There's a piece of advice that shows up constantly in personal finance, usually delivered with real conviction, and it happens to be almost entirely useless. Just be more disciplined. Think before you spend. Exercise a bit more self-control next time.

I want to explain, properly and in some detail, why this advice fails so reliably, because understanding exactly why it fails is what makes the alternative in this chapter actually worth taking seriously, rather than just another version of the same tired suggestion dressed up in new language.

Why willpower was never going to work

Go back to everything covered across Part Two of this book. Loss aversion, present bias, herding, the endowment effect, social comparison. Every one of those instincts operates below the level of conscious deliberation, firing automatically, in the moment, well before your slower, more careful thinking has a chance to get involved at all. Asking yourself to simply resist them through willpower is a bit like asking yourself to consciously slow your own heart rate through concentration alone. You can try. Some people, in narrow circumstances, briefly succeed. Almost nobody sustains it reliably, day after day, across every single decision where it would actually matter, for months and years on end.

There's a further problem, and it's one that makes willpower an even worse strategy than it first appears. A reasonably large body of research on self-control suggests that resisting temptation draws on a limited resource, one that depletes across the day the more it gets used. Resist the urge to check your phone during an important meeting, resist a colleague's suggestion to skip your lunchtime walk, resist an unnecessary purchase on the way home, and by the time you're standing at the till later that evening, genuinely tired and genuinely depleted, the exact moment a present biased impulse purchase or a loss averse upsell is most likely to catch you, your capacity to resist it has already been spent elsewhere on things that had nothing to do with money at all. Willpower isn't just unreliable. It's unreliable in a way that predictably fails you precisely when you need it most, at the end of a long, effortful day, rather than at the start of a fresh one.

This is precisely why systems work so much better, and it's worth being specific about the mechanism rather than just asserting it. A system doesn't ask you to resist a temptation in the moment at all. It removes the moment of temptation from your path entirely, arranging your financial life so the choice you'd want to make with a full tank of willpower simply happens automatically, without ever requiring you to summon any willpower in the first place.

The automatic saver

Here's a worked example, in proper detail, because the principle only becomes genuinely useful once you can see exactly how it applies in practice.

Recall the postponed saving pattern from Chapter Six, the sentence I'll start saving properly once I'm earning a bit more, endlessly deferred to a future self who never quite arrives at the moment of decision. A willpower based fix asks you to actively decide, every single month, to move money into savings before spending the rest, a decision your present biased brain will reliably deprioritise against whatever feels more urgent that particular month.

A systems based fix removes that monthly decision entirely. Money moves into savings automatically, on payday, before it ever reaches the account you actually spend from, arranged once, as a single decision made with a full tank of willpower on a calm day, rather than repeated every month under whatever pressure that month happens to bring. This is sometimes described, in the research literature, as paying yourself first, and the evidence behind it is genuinely strong. Programmes built around exactly this principle, automatically escalating a saver's contribution rate over time rather than asking them to actively choose a higher rate each year, have produced dramatically higher savings rates than programmes relying on active, repeated, willpower-based decisions. The mechanism doing the work isn't motivation. It's the simple fact that the decision only ever needs to be made once.

Notice something important about why this specifically defeats present bias rather than merely working around it. The decision to save is made today, by a present self who, in this one specific moment, is thinking about the future rather than discounting it. Every month after that, no further decision is required at all. The future self who might otherwise have deprioritised saving that particular month never actually gets asked to make the choice. They have already been overridden by an earlier version of themself who happened to be feeling more far sighted.

The size limit that removes the anchor

Here's a second worked example, this one aimed squarely at the anchoring problem from Chapter Nine, the one bias we established doesn't come from ancient wiring at all and is entirely our own modern invention.

A willpower-based defence against anchoring asks you to consciously notice, every single time, that a reduced from price or a first quoted figure is shaping your judgement, and to deliberately set that number aside before deciding what something is actually worth to you. This is exhausting to do consistently, and most people, most of the time, simply won't manage it, not through any personal failing but because it asks conscious effort at precisely the moment an anchor has already done its quiet work, often before you've even noticed a number was shown to you at all.

A systems based defence works differently, and considerably more reliably. Before entering any negotiation, or before browsing for any significant purchase, decide on your own number first, based on independent research into what something is actually worth, completely separate from whatever number a seller or advertisement is about to show you. Write it down if that helps make it concrete. Only then look at the seller's price, the reduced from figure, the anchor being offered. Because your own number was fixed before the anchor ever entered the picture, it has nothing left to shift. The anchor still gets shown to you. It simply arrives too late to do its work, because the number it would otherwise have shifted was already locked in beforehand.

Friction, deliberately added back in

Not every system works by removing a decision. Sometimes the more useful system works by deliberately adding a small amount of friction back into a decision that's currently far too easy, precisely because ease is exactly what a monkey brain responds to most readily.

Recall the four easy payments from Chapter Six and Chapter Twelve, and the extended warranty offered at the till in Chapter Eleven, both designed, whether deliberately or through the feedback loop covered in Chapter Ten, to make a purchase decision feel as effortless as possible in the moment it's made. A useful personal system here is a simple, fixed rule, decided in advance, on a calm day, rather than negotiated fresh each time. Any purchase over a certain size waits twenty four hours before being confirmed. Not because twenty four hours changes the facts of the purchase, but because it reliably removes the purchase from the exact moment your present biased, momentum carried brain was most persuaded, and hands the final decision instead to a version of you thinking somewhat more clearly the following day.

This works for precisely the same reason automatic saving works, just aimed in the opposite direction. Rather than removing a decision entirely, it deliberately relocates the decision away from the moment your monkey is most active, and toward a moment when your slower, more deliberate thinking actually gets a fair say in the outcome.

The pre-written sell rule

One further system, aimed at loss aversion specifically, the bias this whole book opened with. A willpower-based defence asks you to decide, in the moment, whether a falling investment has genuinely stopped being worth holding, precisely the moment loss aversion is working hardest to keep you attached to it. A systems-based defence writes the rule before the fall ever happens, a fixed condition, decided on a calm day with no losses currently in play, under which you'll review or exit a position, agreed with yourself in writing rather than negotiated fresh in the anxious moment a price starts dropping. The rule doesn't need to be complicated to work. It simply needs to exist before the moment it's meant to govern, so the decision it makes was never really made under pressure at all.

The common thread

Look at the automatic saver, the pre-decided number, the twenty four hour rule, and the pre-written sell rule together, and a single principle runs through all four. None of them ask you to be a stronger, more disciplined version of yourself in the heat of the moment. All four accept, honestly and without judgement, that the heat of the moment belongs to your monkey, and arrange things instead so the moment that actually matters, the one where the real decision gets locked in, happens somewhere else entirely, at a point where a calmer, more far-sighted version of you was already in charge.

That's the whole discipline this final part of the book is built on. Not willpower, which fails predictably and at the worst possible time. Systems, built once, on a good day, that quietly keep working on all the bad days you haven't had yet.

CHAPTER 14

BUILDING YOUR OWN GUARDRAILS

The last chapter made the case for systems over willpower in general terms. This one gets specific. I want to hand you a genuine toolkit here, not a vague sense that automation is a good idea, but a set of concrete guardrails you could actually put in place this week, each one aimed at a particular monkey from Part Two, built to intercept him before he gets anywhere near your money.

Naming the moment before it arrives

Every guardrail in this chapter shares a common structure worth understanding before we get into the specifics. A guardrail works by identifying, in advance, on a calm day, the exact moment a particular bias is most likely to strike, and building something into that precise moment that either removes the decision entirely or slows it down enough for your more deliberate thinking to catch up.

This matters because a vague intention to be more

careful with money doesn't specify a moment at all, which is exactly why it fails so reliably. Your monkey doesn't announce himself in advance. He shows up disguised as a perfectly reasonable urge, at a perfectly ordinary moment, and a guardrail only works if it's already sitting there waiting for him when he arrives.

The separate account for the vivid loss

Chapter Three covered the pattern of over-insuring against vivid, easily imagined losses while under-insuring against larger, statistically real ones. Here's a concrete guardrail that addresses both halves of that pattern at once, rather than just the first half most people instinctively reach for.

Before considering any specific insurance product, whether an extended warranty, travel cover, or gadget insurance, ask a single fixed question, written down somewhere you'll actually see it again. What is the maximum amount I could genuinely lose here, and could I comfortably absorb that loss from savings without meaningful hardship. If the honest answer is yes, you can absorb it, the insurance is very likely priced to favour the insurer rather than you, on average, across enough customers, and self-insuring, simply setting aside a small equivalent amount each month into a general reserve rather than paying for cover on every individual item, will very likely leave you better off over time. If the honest answer is no, you genuinely couldn't absorb the loss, that's precisely the guardrail's real value, because it will also catch the income protection or life insurance conversation most people never have, the one covering a genuinely large, statistically real risk that never got flagged with the same urgency a cracked phone screen manages effortlessly. The same single question, applied consistently, corrects both sides of the pattern that Chapter Three described.

The cooling off rule, properly specified

Chapter Thirteen introduced the idea of a fixed waiting period before larger purchases. Worth being considerably more specific here about how to actually build this, because a vague intention to wait fails for exactly the same reason a vague intention to save more does.

Pick a threshold in advance, calibrated to your own finances rather than borrowed from someone else's, the kind of amount that would genuinely register if lost but wouldn't be catastrophic. Any purchase above that threshold, without exception, gets written down rather than bought immediately, and revisited after a fixed period, several days works better than a single day, since a single day still sits close enough to the original momentum to barely count. If the purchase still feels genuinely worthwhile once that period has passed, buy it, with a clear conscience and considerably more confidence than an impulse purchase could ever have offered. If the appeal has quietly faded, and for a striking number of purchases it will have, you've just avoided exactly the kind of loss aversion driven, momentum carried decision covered across Part Two, without ever having to rely on willpower in the moment itself.

One detail that makes the guardrail considerably more robust, is deciding in advance that the rule applies without exception, including to purchases that feel like they don't need it. The moment you feel most tempted to skip the waiting period, telling yourself this particular purchase is different, obviously sensible, too good an opportunity to delay, is almost always exactly the moment the rule was built to catch in the first place.

The rebalancing date that ignores the news

Chapter Seven covered the endowment effect and the reluctance to rebalance a portfolio simply because its current contents already feel like mine. Chapter Five covered herding, chasing whatever's performed well recently. Here's a single guardrail that defends against both at once.

Choose a fixed date, once or twice a year, entirely disconnected from any market news, a birthday or the start of a new tax year works well simply because it has no emotional connection to any specific investment decision. On that date, and only on that date, review your portfolio against your original intended allocation, and rebalance back toward it, regardless of what's currently performing well or badly, regardless of what feels uncomfortable to sell or difficult to justify holding onto. The discipline here isn't reacting faster to markets. It's deliberately reacting slower, on a schedule chosen in advance rather than in response to whatever headline or neighbour's success happens to be triggering an urge to act right now.

• • •

The pre-decided answer to family and friends

One guardrail doesn't map onto a single chapter so much as the general pull of social proof covered in Chapter Five and Chapter Eight. Financial requests and suggestions from people close to you, a relative pushing an investment, a friend suggesting you join them in some new venture, carry weight that has nothing to do with the merits of the suggestion itself and everything to do with who's making it.

The useful guardrail here is a prepared, standard response, decided in advance rather than improvised under social pressure in the moment. Something close to, that sounds interesting, let me look into it properly and get back to you. Said calmly, without needing to justify it further, this buys exactly the same distance from social pressure that the cooling off rule buys from purchase momentum, and it works for the same underlying reason. The pressure to decide immediately, out loud, in front of the person making the suggestion, is doing almost all of the persuasive work. Remove the immediacy, and the suggestion has to stand or fall on its actual merits instead.

The independent number, written down first

One final guardrail, aimed squarely at anchoring, the one bias Chapter Nine established has no ancient excuse attached to it at all, which makes it, in a sense, the guardrail with the least room for self-forgiveness if it's skipped.

Before entering any negotiation, or before seriously considering any significant purchase, price, quote or offer, do the research and arrive at your own independent number first, based purely on comparable evidence, before you ever see the seller's figure. Write it down, somewhere physical if that helps make it feel properly committed rather than a vague impression you can quietly revise later. Only once that number exists should you look at whatever price, discount or comparison the other party is presenting. Because your own figure was fixed before the anchor arrived, the anchor has nothing left to move. It can still be shown to you, the reduced from price, the first number mentioned, the competitor comparison chosen by someone else. It simply arrives too late to do the work it was built to do, because the number it would otherwise have quietly shifted was already locked in beforehand.

Build this guardrail genuinely into everything with real financial weight: a mortgage rate, a car purchase, a salary negotiation, precisely because anchoring is silent and fast, doing its work in the moment a number is first seen, well before your slower thinking has had any chance to intervene. A cooling off period helps against momentum. A rebalancing date helps against inertia and herding. Against anchoring specifically, the only genuinely reliable defence is making sure your own number exists in the world before the seller's number ever gets the chance to shape it.

Building your own set

These six guardrails aren't an exhaustive list, and they're not meant to be applied identically by every reader. The genuinely useful exercise, once you've seen how each one works, is building your own, tailored to whichever chapter landed hardest — the one where maybe you recognised yourself a little too clearly to enjoy it. If Chapter Four's sunk cost material landed hardest, your guardrail might be a fixed rule for reviewing any ongoing project or investment purely on its forward-looking merits, ignoring what's already been spent, on a schedule rather than only when a nagging doubt happens to surface. If Chapter Six's present bias chapter hit closest to home, automating your saving the way Chapter Thirteen described is probably the single highest value guardrail available to you.

The common thread, one final time, is that every genuinely effective guardrail is built once, in advance, on a calm day, and aimed precisely at the moment your particular monkey is most likely to show up. Build it well, and you'll rarely even notice it working. You'll simply notice, some months or years later, that the mistakes covered in Part Two of this book have started happening to you considerably less often than they used to.

CHAPTER 15
BECOMING A HARDER TARGET

You're sitting across a desk, or a screen, from someone selling you something that fits your wiring unusually well. That's not automatically a reason for alarm. It's a reason to look closely. This final chapter of Part Four turns outward one more time, back to the products and marketing covered in Part Three, and asks a genuinely practical question: now that you understand how a design ends up shaped the way it is — feedback loop rather than conspiracy — what specifically do you do about it?

Recognising the shape, not hunting for villains

I want to return briefly to the distinction Chapter Ten drew, because it matters enormously for how this chapter's advice should actually be used. The goal here isn't developing a permanent suspicion of every financial product or every person selling one, treating each interaction as an adversarial encounter with a hidden enemy. Most people building and selling these products are, as Chapter Ten argued at length, simply doing their jobs, working with designs that survived because they converted, not designs built with malicious intent.

The goal instead is recognising shape. A product or a pitch that happens to fit your wiring unusually well isn't automatically bad, but it deserves exactly the same scrutiny you'd give it if it fit your wiring poorly, and that scrutiny is precisely what tends to go missing the moment something feels unusually easy to say yes to.

The questions worth asking, and why each one works

Here's a genuine, practical checklist, built directly from the biases covered across Part Two, each question aimed at defusing one specific instinct before it gets to make the decision for you.

Would I still want this if I'd found it myself, rather than had it presented to me. This targets the herding instinct from Chapter Five directly. A recommendation from an adviser, a friend, or an advertisement carries persuasive weight entirely separate from the merits of the thing being recommended, and this question strips that borrowed weight away, asking you to evaluate the substance on its own rather than on the strength of who's currently vouching for it.

What is this price being compared against, and did I choose that comparison myself. This targets anchoring, covered properly in Chapter Nine as the one genuinely human, rather than ancient, vulnerability in this entire book. A reduced from figure, a competitor comparison chosen by the seller rather than by you, a first number mentioned in a negotiation, all of it is doing quiet work shaping what feels reasonable. Asking where the comparison came from, and insisting on choosing your own instead, based on independent research rather than whatever figure you were shown, is the single most direct defence against a bias with no evolutionary excuse attached to it at all.

What happens if I do nothing right now. This targets the artificial urgency covered in Chapter Twelve. A genuinely time limited opportunity survives this question easily, because the honest answer will be that a real deadline genuinely does cost you something by waiting. A manufactured deadline, the kind designed purely to collapse your careful thinking into quick instinct, tends to reveal itself the moment you actually sit with the question, because in the overwhelming majority of cases, the honest answer is that very little happens at all, and the same or a similar offer reappears again before long regardless.

Am I about to lose something real, or just something I've already decided I'm entitled to. This targets loss aversion from Chapter Three directly, and it's worth sitting with, because the wording matters. A genuine loss is a real, material reduction in what you currently have. A merely imagined loss, the kind an insurance add-on or a limited time offer often trades on, is the loss of an opportunity you never actually possessed in the first place, dressed up to feel exactly like the real thing. Your monkey can't easily tell the difference between the two in the moment. This question exists precisely to do that work for him.

Would I make the same decision if I'd had to write down my own number first. This targets the same anchoring problem from a slightly different angle, and it directly echoes the pre-decided number guardrail from Chapter Fourteen. If you genuinely arrived at your own independent figure before seeing the seller's price, and the two happen to align, that's a coincidence worth trusting. If you skipped straight to reacting to the seller's price without ever forming your own view first, the alignment, if there is any, tells you nothing at all about whether the price is actually fair.

A worked example, start to finish

Here's how these questions actually apply together, rather than leaving them as an abstract list, because the real value shows up when several of them get asked in sequence against a single genuine decision.

Imagine you're offered a limited time upgrade on a financial product you already hold, a better rate, available only if you act within a stated window, recommended enthusiastically by the person presenting it. Run the checklist properly. Would you want this if you'd found it yourself, researching independently, rather than had it pitched to you in this specific moment. What is the improved rate being compared against, and is that comparison one you chose or one you were handed. What genuinely happens if you say you'll think about it and come back tomorrow, rather than deciding right now. Is there a real, material loss on the table if you wait, or only the loss of a deadline that was manufactured specifically to make waiting feel costly. And if you'd worked out independently, before this conversation ever started, what a genuinely good rate would look like, does this offer actually clear that bar, or does it only look good relative to whatever number was shown alongside it.

Run through all five honestly, and you'll very often find the decision either holds up cleanly, in which case proceed with real confidence rather than lingering doubt, or it quietly falls apart the moment the borrowed urgency and the borrowed comparison get stripped away, revealing a decision that was never actually as good as it felt in the room.

A second worked example, further up the stakes

Worth running through the same checklist once more, this time against a considerably larger decision, because the pattern holds regardless of scale, and seeing it applied twice makes the habit easier to carry into whatever situation you actually face.

Imagine you're viewing a house, and the estate agent mentions, entirely truthfully, that there's another viewing booked straight after yours, and interest has been strong all week. The property sits at the very top of what you'd budgeted, and something in the pit of your stomach starts pushing you toward an offer before you've even left the driveway. Run the same five questions. Would you still want this house at this price if you'd found it yourself, cold, with no queue on the pavement and no agent mentioning other interested buyers. What is your sense of a fair price actually being compared against, the asking price the seller chose, or a number you worked out independently from genuinely comparable sales nearby. What actually happens if you leave today, sleep on it, and make a considered offer tomorrow morning instead of a rushed one this afternoon, and is that consequence a real, material loss of the property, or only the loss of being first in a queue that may not even determine who the seller ultimately chooses. Is the discomfort you're feeling a response to a genuine, well evidenced risk of missing out, or simply the vivid, uncomfortable feeling of watching someone else potentially get something you've decided you want. And if you'd written down, before this viewing, exactly what you were prepared to pay based on your own research, does today's number still hold, or has the room itself just talked you into a figure your calmer, better informed self never actually agreed to.

Asked properly, in order, these five questions rarely change a genuinely good decision. What they reliably do is catch the decision that was never actually about the house at all, and was really about the queue on the pavement, the same instinct covered fully back in Chapter Five, dressed up in a considerably more expensive outfit than it wore the first time you met it.

The point of all of this

None of the five questions in this chapter require you to distrust the person sitting across from you, or to treat every financial interaction as a battle to be won. Most of the time, as Chapter Ten argued, there's no adversary there at all, simply a product and a pitch shaped, over years, by what happened to convert. What these questions actually do is considerably more modest and considerably more useful. They slow the specific moment down just long enough for the version of you that isn't a monkey to actually get a vote in the decision, rather than watching the vote get cast entirely on his behalf, in the split second before you'd normally have said yes.

That's the whole of Part Four, in the end. Not becoming a harder, more suspicious person. Becoming someone who's simply built a few small, deliberate pauses into exactly the moments that used to belong entirely to instinct.

CONCLUSION

Conclusion: You're Not Broken, You're Just a Monkey With a Bank Account

Go back to the very first page of this book for a moment. You'd done something stupid with money. So had I. So has everyone standing anywhere near either of us. That was the whole premise, and I want to return to it now, because I think it means something rather different at the end of this book than it did at the beginning.

At the start, that sentence was meant to be a relief. A permission slip. You're not uniquely careless, uniquely undisciplined, uniquely bad with money. You're simply running old software on hardware built for an entirely different job, and a great deal of what felt like personal failure was never really that at all. I stand by every word of that, and if it's the only thing you take from this book, it's still a genuinely useful thing to carry forward.

But it was never meant to be the whole story, and I hope by now it doesn't read as one.

What the four parts actually add up to

Part One told you where your monkey came from, a brain finished long before money, mortgages or pensions existed, still running the only playbook it's ever had. Part Two took you through that monkey in action, loss aversion, sunk cost, herding, present bias, the endowment effect, social comparison, each one tested and confirmed in creatures who've never seen a bank statement, proof that none of it was taught to you so much as inherited. And then, right in the middle, Chapter Nine drew a line I hope you've held onto since. Not everything is the monkey. Anchoring isn't. Financial illiteracy isn't. Some of what trips you up is simply information nobody explained properly, or a piece of cognitive machinery that belongs to you specifically as a modern human, with no ancient excuse attached to it at all.

Part Three turned that same understanding outward, toward the products and marketing you encounter every day, not to hand you a villain, but to show you a second monkey, standing on the other side of the counter, building and selling things shaped by exactly the same feedback loop that shapes your own decisions. And Part Four, finally, gave you something to actually do with all of it. Not willpower, which fails predictably and at the worst possible moment. Systems, guardrails, and a handful of honest questions, built once, on a calm day, and left waiting for exactly the moments your monkey used to have entirely to himself.

The reframe that was the whole point

Here's the sentence I'd like you to leave with, because it's the one that ties all four parts together properly. Understanding the wiring doesn't excuse a bad decision. It explains it, and explanation is the first genuinely useful step toward doing something about it. A pilot who understands turbulence still has to fly the plane through it. But a pilot who doesn't understand it at all is flying blind, reacting to every jolt as though it's uniquely personal, uniquely alarming, uniquely their own failure to keep the aircraft steady. You are no longer that pilot. You now know exactly what the turbulence is, roughly when it's coming, and precisely which instruments actually help you fly through it steadily.

That knowledge won't make the monkey disappear. Nobody manages that, and I'd be lying to you on the very last page if I suggested otherwise. You will still feel the pull to sell in a panic, to hold on to something failing simply because you've already put so much in, to want whatever your neighbour just bought, to promise, once again, that you'll start saving properly next month. The wiring is a few hundred thousand years old. This book was never going to switch it off in an afternoon's reading.

What it will do, if you've actually taken in the chapters behind you rather than just read past them, is change the speed at which you recognise him. He'll show up, wallet in hand, absolutely certain of himself, the way he always has. But you'll catch the shape of him a little faster now. You'll recognise the vivid loss dressed up to look more urgent than the statistics justify. You'll notice the deadline that was never really about time. You'll feel the pull of a number you didn't choose, and remember to ask where it actually came from.

Go back, for a moment, to that Tuesday evening from Chapter One, the phone notification about a small market dip landing with real force, the unopened pension statement sitting quietly in a drawer, entirely unable to compete for your attention. Imagine that same evening happening again, sometime after you've properly finished this book. The notification still arrives. It probably always will, because a portfolio moving slightly is simply what portfolios do, and no amount of insight changes what your monkey feels when a number briefly turns red. But you now know exactly what that small tightening in your chest actually is, an old, well documented, thoroughly tested piece of wiring reacting to visibility rather than to genuine risk, and knowing that changes what you do next. You check the notification, recognise the monkey for what he is, and close the app. The pension statement, meanwhile, might finally get opened, not because the urge to check it has grown any stronger on its own, but because you've built a system, a fixed date, a standing reminder, that no longer depends on urge at all. That's the whole shift this book has been arguing for, in miniature. Not louder alarm bells for the things that matter. Quieter, more accurate ones for the things that don't, and a system standing in for attention where attention was never going to show up reliably on its own.

What to do next

If you want a single next step, and only one, make it this. Go back to whichever chapter in Part Two made you wince hardest, the one where you recognised yourself a little too clearly, and build the guardrail for it this week, not eventually, not once you've finished reading every book on the shelf about this, this week, while the recognition is still fresh enough to actually act on. One automatic transfer set up. One waiting period rule written down. One prepared answer for the next time a friend or relative pitches you something across a table. Small, boring, built once. That's the entire method this book has been arguing for since Part Four began, and it works precisely because it doesn't ask anything more dramatic of you than that.

You picked this book up because you'd done something stupid with money, the same as everyone else has. I hope you're putting it down with something more useful than shame about that. Not a cure. Nobody manages that. Just a clearer view of exactly who's been standing behind the wheel all along, and a genuinely fair chance, from here on, of sharing the driving with him instead of simply handing over the keys every single time he asks. Drive safely. He means well. He just doesn't always know the road.

REFERENCES

Notes and Sources

This book leans heavily on real, published research, and I wanted to give you a proper way to look any of it up for yourself, rather than simply asking you to take my word for it. What follows isn't a full academic bibliography, just enough detail to find each study if you're curious, organised by the chapter where it appears.

A few of these findings are genuinely contested by other researchers, and I've noted that honestly wherever it applies, because a book asking for your trust should be straightforward about where the evidence gets argued over by the people who produced it.

The Brain You Didn't Choose

Blanchard, T. C., & Hayden, B. Y. (2015). "Monkeys Are More Patient in a Foraging Task than in a Standard Intertemporal Choice Task." PLOS ONE. General evidence that delay discounting in primates behaves differently depending on context, used here as background for the idea that discounting is an old, evolved trait rather than a modern character flaw.

The Monkey Marketplace

Chen, M. K., Lakshminarayanan, V., & Santos, L. R. (2006). "How Basic Are Behavioral Biases? Evidence from Capuchin Monkey Trading Behavior." Journal of Political Economy, 114(3), 517–537. This is the central study behind the whole book, the Yale "monkey marketplace" research establishing that capuchins display loss aversion, the reflection effect, and the endowment effect after being taught to trade tokens for food.

Chen, M. K., Lakshminarayanan, V., & Santos, L. R. "The Evolution of Our Preferences: Evidence from Capuchin-Monkey Trading Behaviour." Cowles Foundation Discussion Paper No. 1524, Yale University. A related working paper covering the same research programme in more detail.

Lakshminarayanan, V., Chen, M. K., & Santos, L. R. (2008). The follow-up endowment effect study, in which capuchins given a food item to hold showed reduced willingness to trade it for a supposedly equivalent alternative, referenced in Catapano et al. (2014) as part of the same research programme.

The Pain of Losing

Draws on the same Chen, Lakshminarayanan & Santos (2006) findings as Chapter Two, specifically the loss aversion and reflection effect results.

Worth noting honestly: Silberberg, A., Roma, P. G., Huntsberry, M. E., et al. (2008). "On Loss Aversion in

Capuchin Monkeys." Journal of the Experimental Analysis of Behavior, 89(2), 145–155. This paper reanalyses the original data and argues the monkeys' behaviour may be better explained by delay of reinforcement rather than genuine loss aversion. The debate between these interpretations hasn't been fully settled, and I've flagged this openly in the chapter itself.

Throwing Good Money After Bad

Blanchard, T. C., Hayden, B. Y., et al. (2020). "Capuchin and rhesus monkeys show sunk cost effects in a psychomotor task." Scientific Reports. The study behind the sunk cost material in this chapter, including the detail that rhesus macaques showed the effect more strongly than capuchins.

Worth noting honestly: a rebuttal published in Science Advances argues that apparent sunk cost effects in animals can sometimes be explained by a rational, uncertainty-resolving strategy rather than a true fallacy. I've reflected this open debate in the chapter's "honest complication" section.

Everybody's Doing It

Canteloup, C., et al. (2020). "Wild primates copy higher-ranked individuals in a social transmission experiment." Nature Communications. The vervet monkey study showing social learning and a rank-based transmission bias.

van de Waal, E., et al. The "blue versus pink maize" field study on wild vervet monkeys, documenting how migrating males rapidly adopted their new troop's local food colour preference. Widely reported, including in Scientific American.

Tomorrow Never Comes

Blanchard & Hayden (2015), as cited in Chapter One, provides general evidence for delay discounting in primates.

Keith Chen, quoted in Stanford Magazine ("Monkey Business"), on capuchins being unlikely to ever learn to save money due to limited impulse control.

Worth noting honestly: research on the "conditioning-delay gradient" argues that some apparent delay discounting in monkeys may reflect a memory or conditioning artefact rather than pure impatience. I've presented both explanations in the chapter as an open question with different practical implications.

Mine Is Better Because It's Mine

Lakshminarayanan, Chen & Santos (2008), the endowment effect follow-up study introduced in Chapter Two, is the primary evidence here.

Keeping Up with the Troop

Brosnan, S. F., & de Waal, F. B. M. (2003). "Monkeys reject unequal pay." Nature, 425, 297–299. The original cucumber-and-grape capuchin fairness study.

Brosnan, S. F., & de Waal, F. B. M. (2004). "Fair refusal by capuchin monkeys." Nature, 428, 140. A follow-up reply defending the original interpretation against critics.

Worth noting honestly: Wynne, C. D. L. (2004). "Inequity aversion in capuchins?" Nature, 428, 139. This response disputes the fairness interpretation, arguing the monkeys' reaction may reflect simple frustration at a visible, unattained reward rather than genuine reasoning about fairness between two parties. I've noted in the chapter that the practical takeaway holds regardless of which interpretation is correct.

No Monkey to Be Seen

Catapano, R., Buttrick, N., Widness, J., Goldstein, N., & Santos, L. R. (2014). "Capuchin monkeys do not show human-like pricing effects." Frontiers in Psychology. This is the key evidence for the chapter's central argument, that anchoring, unlike loss aversion and the endowment effect, did not appear in the same capuchin population tested by the same Yale researchers, suggesting it may depend on cognitive machinery unique to humans.

Part Three doesn't draw on primate research, since it concerns product design and marketing rather than evolved psychology. The arguments in these chapters are drawn from my own twenty-five years working across financial services platforms, alongside general, publicly documented industry practice around product testing, fee disclosure, and regulatory obligations requiring firms to evidence fair customer outcomes.

Part Four similarly draws on general behavioural economics and habit-formation research on commitment devices, automation, and friction, rather than primate studies specifically. Readers interested in the research behind automatic saving in particular may want to look up work on automatic enrolment and escalation in retirement saving schemes, a well-documented area showing dramatically higher participation and contribution rates compared with schemes requiring active, repeated decisions.

A final honest note. Behavioural science is a genuinely contested field, and several of the findings in this book have been challenged, refined, or reinterpreted since their original publication. I've tried to flag every major dispute I'm aware of rather than presenting a tidier picture than the evidence actually supports. Where I've simplified a nuanced debate for readability, the fault is mine, and the original papers above are the place to go for the fuller, messier, more interesting picture.

ABOUT THE AUTHOR

Stuart Welch spent twenty-five years working inside the financial services industry, watching from the inside how it talked about money, how it talked to ordinary people, and how wide the gap between the two so often became. He is not a financial adviser. He never sat across a desk telling people where to put their money. What he did was pay close attention — to how the industry worked, what it got right, and what it consistently got wrong and how retail customers behaved.

Educated at the University of Leeds, Stuart has spent much of his career trying to close the distance between the world of finance and the millions of perfectly capable people it too often leaves behind.

The Monkey In Your Wallet is his ninth book. Unlike his previous books which deal more with the how and what of investing, it is a book that leans into why we react to money matters the way we do

Stuart lives in West Yorkshire.

You can read more at www.simpleinvesting.co.uk

ALSO BY THE AUTHOR

Simple Investing For Absolute Beginners

Simple Investing: Sort Out Your Pension

Simple Investing For Retirement

Simple Investing Guide to FIRE

Simple Investing For Women

Simple Investing Guide To Ethical Investing

Simple Investing For The Self-Employed

Simple Investing For People In Their Twenties

See more at: simpleinvesting.co.uk

www.ingramcontent.com/pod-product-compliance
Lightning Source LLC
LaVergne TN
LVHW010727061126
851857LV00014B/1380
* 9 7 8 1 9 1 8 8 5 1 0 4 5 *